ALSO BY ELIZABETH BISHOP

North & South (1946)

A Cold Spring (1955)

The Diary of "Helena Morley" (translation) (1957)

Brazil (with the editors of *Life*) (prose) (1962)

Questions of Travel (1965)

The Ballad of the Burglar of Babylon (1968)

The Complete Poems (1969)

An Anthology of Twentieth-Century Brazilian Poetry
(edited with Emanuel Brasil) (1972)

Geography III (1976)

The Complete Poems, 1927–1979 (1983)

The Collected Prose (edited by Robert Giroux) (1984)

One Art: Letters (edited by Robert Giroux) (1994)

Exchanging Hats: Paintings (edited by William Benton) (1996)

Edgar Allan Poe & The Juke-Box:
Uncollected Poems, Drafts, and Fragments (edited by Alice Quinn) (2006)

Elizabeth Bishop: Poems, Prose, and Letters
(selected by Robert Giroux and Lloyd Schwartz) (2008)

Words in Air: The Complete Correspondence Between
Elizabeth Bishop and Robert Lowell
(edited by Thomas Travisano with Saskia Hamilton) (2008)

Elizabeth Bishop and The New Yorker
(edited by Joelle Biele) (2011)

Prose (edited by Lloyd Schwartz) (2011)

POEMS

POEMS

ELIZABETH BISHOP

FARRAR, STRAUS AND GIROUX   NEW YORK

Farrar, Straus and Giroux
18 West 18th Street, New York 10011

Printed in the United States of America
First edition, 2011

Published simultaneously in hardcover (as part of a two-volume boxed set with
Elizabeth Bishop's *Prose*, edited by Lloyd Schwartz) and in paperback

The facsimile on page 320 appears with the permission of Houghton Library,
Harvard University. The facsimile on page 312 is from a private collection,
photograph courtesy of Carmen Oliveira, with thanks to Barbara Page and
Lloyd Schwartz. The facsimile on page 326 is from the collection of Lloyd
Schwartz. All other facsimiles appear by permission of Special Collections,
Vassar College Libraries, and the Alice H. Methfessel Trust.

Library of Congress Cataloging-in-Publication Data
Bishop, Elizabeth, 1911–1979.
    [Poems. Selections]
    Poems / Elizabeth Bishop. — 1st ed.
        p.   cm.
    Includes index.
    ISBN 978-0-374-12656-8 (cloth : alk. paper)
    ISBN 978-0-374-53236-9 (pbk. : alk. paper)
PS3503.I785A6 2010
811'.54—dc22
                                                    2010038535

Boxed Set ISBN: 978-0-374-12558-5

Designed by Jonathan D. Lippincott

www.fsgbooks.com

11

Acknowledgments

The publisher wishes to acknowledge the following for assistance with research and the preparation of the text: Dean Rogers, Laura Finkel, and Ron Patkus of Vassar College Libraries Special Collections; Leslie Morris, Heather Cole, Rachel Howarth, James Capobianco, Mary Haegert, Susan Halpert, Emilie Hardman, Micah Hoggatt, Emily Walhout, and Joseph Zajac of the Houghton Library, Harvard University; Elizabeth E. Fuller and Karen Schoenewaldt of the Rosenbach Museum and Library; John Cordovez, Nasima Hasnat, Thomas Lannon, and Lee Spilberg of the Manuscripts and Archives Division of the New York Public Library; and Catherine Barnett, Paulo Britto, Eleanor Chai, Frank Bidart, Eamon Grennan, Paul Keegan, Carmen Oliveira, Barbara Page, Alice Quinn, and Lloyd Schwartz. Thanks above all to Saskia Hamilton, for her painstaking care in helping prepare this edition.

Contents

A Cold Spring (1955)

Questions of Travel (1965)

Publisher's Note

This edition of Elizabeth Bishop's poems, printed for the centenary of her birth, includes all the poems and translations she published between 1933 and her death in 1979.* It preserves the distinction Bishop made between poems and translations collected in volumes and those she left out of her books after their appearance in periodicals and anthologies. It follows her selection and arrangement of *The Complete Poems* (1969) and *Geography III* (1976), supplemented by four late poems left uncollected at her death. The other published poems and translations that she chose to omit from her two final volumes are gathered in two parts in a final section.

Bishop recalled that, as a young poet, a visit with Marianne Moore would leave her uplifted and determined "never to try to publish anything until I thought I'd done my best with it, no matter how many years it took—or never to publish at all." The many poems in her archive that were left nearly finished attest to the strength of her resolve. *The Complete Poems* was itself a selection ("Omissions are not accidents," as the epigraph to Marianne Moore's own *Complete Poems* warns). It provided the occasion for Bishop to winnow and revise as she gathered her work. Revisions here included changes to the original ordering and contents of her three collections to date (*North & South*, *A Cold Spring*, and *Questions of Travel*). She offered a selection of her translations of Portuguese poetry, which is integral to the structure of this book (much as "Objects & Apparitions," a translation of a poem by Octavio Paz, is integral to *Geography III*), but excluded earlier translations of French poetry. And she chose to include only three early works ("The Hanging of the Mouse," "Some Dreams They Forgot," and "Song") to accompany recently finished work.

As editions of her poems published since her death have demonstrated, Bishop left behind a large body of other material that she did not feel "I'd done my best with" or "did not finish or publish for other reasons" but which is of unquestionable literary interest. Several poems not published in her lifetime first appeared in cleaned-up transcriptions in the 1983 edition of *The Complete Poems, 1927–1979*. From 1983

---

* The year 1933 has been taken as a point of departure, being the date of the earliest published poem included in Bishop's selection for *The Complete Poems* (1969).

to 2006, books and articles by Bishop scholars quoted and discussed other texts. These and other discoveries were presented and annotated in *Edgar Allan Poe & The Juke-Box* (2006). Still more have appeared since in reviews, and in the Library of America's *Elizabeth Bishop: Poems, Prose, and Letters* (2008).* An appendix to the present volume includes a group of these manuscript poems, which offer readers a view of Bishop's working methods.

A second appendix lists the contents of Elizabeth Bishop's books of poetry as first published from 1946 to 1977.

---

* Even so, the published texts have not exhausted what the archive contains—including manuscript poems and translations as yet unpublished, as well as unpublished drafts of eventually completed and published poems, poems by others, song lyrics (blues, ballads) written down or translated, and notebook entries.

THE COMPLETE POEMS
(1969)

North & South (1946)

The Map

Land lies in water; it is shadowed green.
Shadows, or are they shallows, at its edges
showing the line of long sea-weeded ledges
where weeds hang to the simple blue from green.
Or does the land lean down to lift the sea from under,
drawing it unperturbed around itself?
Along the fine tan sandy shelf
is the land tugging at the sea from under?

The shadow of Newfoundland lies flat and still.
Labrador's yellow, where the moony Eskimo
has oiled it. We can stroke these lovely bays,
under a glass as if they were expected to blossom,
or as if to provide a clean cage for invisible fish.
The names of seashore towns run out to sea,
the names of cities cross the neighboring mountains
—the printer here experiencing the same excitement
as when emotion too far exceeds its cause.
These peninsulas take the water between thumb and finger
like women feeling for the smoothness of yard-goods.

Mapped waters are more quiet than the land is,
lending the land their waves' own conformation:
and Norway's hare runs south in agitation,
profiles investigate the sea, where land is.
Are they assigned, or can the countries pick their colors?
—What suits the character or the native waters best.
Topography displays no favorites; North's as near as West.
More delicate than the historians' are the map-makers' colors.

The Imaginary Iceberg

We'd rather have the iceberg than the ship,
although it meant the end of travel.
Although it stood stock-still like cloudy rock
and all the sea were moving marble.
We'd rather have the iceberg than the ship;
we'd rather own this breathing plain of snow
though the ship's sails were laid upon the sea
as the snow lies undissolved upon the water.
O solemn, floating field,
are you aware an iceberg takes repose
with you, and when it wakes may pasture on your snows?

This is a scene a sailor'd give his eyes for.
The ship's ignored. The iceberg rises
and sinks again; its glassy pinnacles
correct elliptics in the sky.
This is a scene where he who treads the boards
is artlessly rhetorical. The curtain
is light enough to rise on finest ropes
that airy twists of snow provide.
The wits of these white peaks
spar with the sun. Its weight the iceberg dares
upon a shifting stage and stands and stares.

This iceberg cuts its facets from within.
Like jewelry from a grave
it saves itself perpetually and adorns
only itself, perhaps the snows
which so surprise us lying on the sea.
Good-bye, we say, good-bye, the ship steers off
where waves give in to one another's waves
and clouds run in a warmer sky.
Icebergs behoove the soul
(both being self-made from elements least visible)
to see them so: fleshed, fair, erected indivisible.

Casabianca

Love's the boy stood on the burning deck
trying to recite "The boy stood on
the burning deck." Love's the son
    stood stammering elocution
      while the poor ship in flames went down.

Love's the obstinate boy, the ship,
even the swimming sailors, who
would like a schoolroom platform, too,
    or an excuse to stay
      on deck. And love's the burning boy.

The Colder the Air

We must admire her perfect aim,
this huntress of the winter air
whose level weapon needs no sight,
if it were not that everywhere
her game is sure, her shot is right.
The least of us could do the same.

The chalky birds or boats stand still,
reducing her conditions of chance;
air's gallery marks identically
the narrow gallery of her glance.
The target-center in her eye
is equally her aim and will.

Time's in her pocket, ticking loud
on one stalled second. She'll consult
not time nor circumstance. She calls
on atmosphere for her result.
(It is this clock that later falls
in wheels and chimes of leaf and cloud.)

Wading at Wellfleet

In one of the Assyrian wars
a chariot first saw the light
that bore sharp blades around its wheels.

That chariot from Assyria
went rolling down mechanically
to take the warriors by the heels.

A thousand warriors in the sea
could not consider such a war
as that the sea itself contrives

but hasn't put in action yet.
This morning's glitterings reveal
the sea is "all a case of knives."

Lying so close, they catch the sun,
the spokes directed at the shin.
The chariot front is blue and great.

The war rests wholly with the waves:
they try revolving, but the wheels
give way; they will not bear the weight.

Chemin de Fer

Alone on the railroad track
    I walked with pounding heart.
The ties were too close together
    or maybe too far apart.

The scenery was impoverished:
    scrub-pine and oak; beyond
its mingled gray-green foliage
    I saw the little pond

where the dirty hermit lives,
    lie like an old tear
holding onto its injuries
    lucidly year after year.

The hermit shot off his shot-gun
    and the tree by his cabin shook.
Over the pond went a ripple.
    The pet hen went chook-chook.

"Love should be put into action!"
    screamed the old hermit.
Across the pond an echo
    tried and tried to confirm it.

The Gentleman of Shalott

Which eye's his eye?
Which limb lies
next the mirror?
For neither is clearer
nor a different color
than the other,
nor meets a stranger
in this arrangement
of leg and leg and
arm and so on.
To his mind
it's the indication
of a mirrored reflection
somewhere along the line
of what we call the spine.

He felt in modesty
his person was
half looking-glass,
for why should he
be doubled?
The glass must stretch
down his middle,
or rather down the edge.
But he's in doubt
as to which side's in or out
of the mirror.
There's little margin for error,
but there's no proof, either.
And if half his head's reflected,
thought, he thinks, might be affected.

But he's resigned
to such economical design.
If the glass slips
he's in a fix—

only one leg, etc. But
while it stays put
he can walk and run
and his hands can clasp one
another. The uncertainty
he says he
finds exhilarating. He loves
that sense of constant re-adjustment.
He wishes to be quoted as saying at present:
"Half is enough."

Large Bad Picture

Remembering the Strait of Belle Isle or
some northerly harbor of Labrador,
before he became a schoolteacher
a great-uncle painted a big picture.

Receding for miles on either side
into a flushed, still sky
are overhanging pale blue cliffs
hundreds of feet high,

their bases fretted by little arches,
the entrances to caves
running in along the level of a bay
masked by perfect waves.

On the middle of that quiet floor
sits a fleet of small black ships,
square-rigged, sails furled, motionless,
their spars like burnt match-sticks.

And high above them, over the tall cliffs'
semi-translucent ranks,
are scribbled hundreds of fine black birds
hanging in *n*'s in banks.

One can hear their crying, crying,
the only sound there is
except for occasional sighing
as a large aquatic animal breathes.

In the pink light
the small red sun goes rolling, rolling,
round and round and round at the same height
in perpetual sunset, comprehensive, consoling,

while the ships consider it.
Apparently they have reached their destination.
It would be hard to say what brought them there,
commerce or contemplation.

From the Country to the City

The long, long legs,
league-boots of land, that carry the city nowhere,
    nowhere; the lines
that we drive on (satin-stripes on harlequin's
    trousers, tights);
his tough trunk dressed in tatters, scribbled over with
    nonsensical signs;
his shadowy, tall dunce-cap; and, best of all his
    shows and sights,
his brain appears, throned in "fantastic triumph,"
    and shines through his hat
with jeweled works at work at intermeshing crowns,
    lamé with lights.
As we approach, wickedest clown, your heart and head,
    we can see that
glittering arrangement of your brain consists, now,
    of mermaid-like,
seated, ravishing sirens, each waving her hand-mirror;
    and we start at
series of slight disturbances up in the telephone wires
    on the turnpike.
Flocks of short, shining wires seem to be flying sidewise.
    Are they birds?
They flash again. No. They are vibrations of the tuning-fork
    you hold and strike
against the mirror-frames, then draw for miles, your dreams,
    out countrywards.
We bring a message from the long black length of body:
    "Subside," it begs and begs.

The Man-Moth*

Here, above,
cracks in the buildings are filled with battered moonlight.
The whole shadow of Man is only as big as his hat.
It lies at his feet like a circle for a doll to stand on,
and he makes an inverted pin, the point magnetized to the moon.
He does not see the moon; he observes only her vast properties,
feeling the queer light on his hands, neither warm nor cold,
of a temperature impossible to record in thermometers.

But when the Man-Moth
pays his rare, although occasional, visits to the surface,
the moon looks rather different to him. He emerges
from an opening under the edge of one of the sidewalks
and nervously begins to scale the faces of the buildings.
He thinks the moon is a small hole at the top of the sky,
proving the sky quite useless for protection.
He trembles, but must investigate as high as he can climb.

Up the façades,
his shadow dragging like a photographer's cloth behind him,
he climbs fearfully, thinking that this time he will manage
to push his small head through that round clean opening
and be forced through, as from a tube, in black scrolls on the light.
(Man, standing below him, has no such illusions.)
But what the Man-Moth fears most he must do, although
he fails, of course, and falls back scared but quite unhurt.

Then he returns
to the pale subways of cement he calls his home. He flits,
he flutters, and cannot get aboard the silent trains
fast enough to suit him. The doors close swiftly.
The Man-Moth always seats himself facing the wrong way
and the train starts at once at its full, terrible speed,

*Newspaper misprint for "mammoth."

without a shift in gears or a gradation of any sort.
He cannot tell the rate at which he travels backwards.

   Each night he must
be carried through artificial tunnels and dream recurrent dreams.
Just as the ties recur beneath his train, these underlie
his rushing brain. He does not dare look out the window,
for the third rail, the unbroken draught of poison,
runs there beside him. He regards it as a disease
he has inherited the susceptibility to. He has to keep
his hands in his pockets, as others must wear mufflers.

   If you catch him,
hold up a flashlight to his eye. It's all dark pupil,
an entire night itself, whose haired horizon tightens
as he stares back, and closes up the eye. Then from the lids
one tear, his only possession, like the bee's sting, slips.
Slyly he palms it, and if you're not paying attention
he'll swallow it. However, if you watch, he'll hand it over,
cool as from underground springs and pure enough to drink.

Love Lies Sleeping

Earliest morning, switching all the tracks
that cross the sky from cinder star to star,
    coupling the ends of streets
    to trains of light,

now draw us into daylight in our beds;
and clear away what presses on the brain:
    put out the neon shapes
    that float and swell and glare

down the gray avenue between the eyes
in pinks and yellows, letters and twitching signs.
    Hang-over moons, wane, wane!
    From the window I see

an immense city, carefully revealed,
made delicate by over-workmanship,
    detail upon detail,
    cornice upon façade

reaching so languidly up into
a weak white sky, it seems to waver there.
    (Where it has slowly grown
    in skies of water-glass

from fused beads of iron and copper crystals,
the little chemical "garden" in a jar
    trembles and stands again,
    pale blue, blue-green, and brick.)

The sparrows hurriedly begin their play.
Then, in the West, "Boom!" and a cloud of smoke.
    "Boom!" and the exploding ball
    of blossom blooms again.

(And all the employees who work in plants
where such a sound says "Danger," or once said "Death,"
    turn in their sleep and feel
    the short hairs bristling

on backs of necks.) The cloud of smoke moves off.
A shirt is taken off a threadlike clothes-line.
    Along the street below
    the water-wagon comes

throwing its hissing, snowy fan across
peelings and newspapers. The water dries
    light-dry, dark-wet, the pattern
    of the cool watermelon.

I hear the day-springs of the morning strike
from stony walls and halls and iron beds,
    scattered or grouped cascades,
    alarms for the expected:

queer cupids of all persons getting up,
whose evening meal they will prepare all day,
    you will dine well
    on his heart, on his, and his,

so send them about your business affectionately,
dragging in the streets their unique loves.
    Scourge them with roses only,
    be light as helium,

for always to one, or several, morning comes,
whose head has fallen over the edge of his bed,
    whose face is turned
    so that the image of

the city grows down into his open eyes
inverted and distorted. No. I mean
    distorted and revealed,
    if he sees it at all.

A Miracle for Breakfast

At six o'clock we were waiting for coffee,
waiting for coffee and the charitable crumb
that was going to be served from a certain balcony,
—like kings of old, or like a miracle.
It was still dark. One foot of the sun
steadied itself on a long ripple in the river.

The first ferry of the day had just crossed the river.
It was so cold we hoped that the coffee
would be very hot, seeing that the sun
was not going to warm us; and that the crumb
would be a loaf each, buttered, by a miracle.
At seven a man stepped out on the balcony.

He stood for a minute alone on the balcony
looking over our heads toward the river.
A servant handed him the makings of a miracle,
consisting of one lone cup of coffee
and one roll, which he proceeded to crumb,
his head, so to speak, in the clouds—along with the sun.

Was the man crazy? What under the sun
was he trying to do, up there on his balcony!
Each man received one rather hard crumb,
which some flicked scornfully into the river,
and, in a cup, one drop of the coffee.
Some of us stood around, waiting for the miracle.

I can tell what I saw next; it was not a miracle.
A beautiful villa stood in the sun
and from its doors came the smell of hot coffee.
In front, a baroque white plaster balcony
added by birds, who nest along the river,
—I saw it with one eye close to the crumb—

and galleries and marble chambers. My crumb
my mansion, made for me by a miracle,
through ages, by insects, birds, and the river
working the stone. Every day, in the sun,
at breakfast time I sit on my balcony
with my feet up, and drink gallons of coffee.

We licked up the crumb and swallowed the coffee.
A window across the river caught the sun
as if the miracle were working, on the wrong balcony.

The Weed

I dreamed that dead, and meditating,
I lay upon a grave, or bed,
(at least, some cold and close-built bower).
In the cold heart, its final thought
stood frozen, drawn immense and clear,
stiff and idle as I was there;
and we remained unchanged together
for a year, a minute, an hour.
Suddenly there was a motion,
as startling, there, to every sense
as an explosion. Then it dropped
to insistent, cautious creeping
in the region of the heart,
prodding me from desperate sleep.
I raised my head. A slight young weed
had pushed up through the heart and its
green head was nodding on the breast.
(All this was in the dark.)
It grew an inch like a blade of grass;
next, one leaf shot out of its side
a twisting, waving flag, and then
two leaves moved like a semaphore.
The stem grew thick. The nervous roots
reached to each side; the graceful head
changed its position mysteriously,
since there was neither sun nor moon
to catch its young attention.
The rooted heart began to change
(not beat) and then it split apart
and from it broke a flood of water.
Two rivers glanced off from the sides,
one to the right, one to the left,
two rushing, half-clear streams,
(the ribs made of them two cascades)
which assuredly, smooth as glass,
went off through the fine black grains of earth.

The weed was almost swept away;
it struggled with its leaves,
lifting them fringed with heavy drops.
A few drops fell upon my face
and in my eyes, so I could see
(or, in that black place, thought I saw)
that each drop contained a light,
a small, illuminated scene;
the weed-deflected stream was made
itself of racing images.
(As if a river should carry all
the scenes that it had once reflected
shut in its waters, and not floating
on momentary surfaces.)
The weed stood in the severed heart.
"What are you doing there?" I asked.
It lifted its head all dripping wet
(with my own thoughts?)
and answered then: "I grow," it said,
"but to divide your heart again."

The Unbeliever

He sleeps on the top of a mast.   —Bunyan

He sleeps on the top of a mast
with his eyes fast closed.
The sails fall away below him
like the sheets of his bed,
leaving out in the air of the night the sleeper's head.

Asleep he was transported there,
asleep he curled
in a gilded ball on the mast's top,
or climbed inside
a gilded bird, or blindly seated himself astride.

"I am founded on marble pillars,"
said a cloud. "I never move.
See the pillars there in the sea?"
Secure in introspection
he peers at the watery pillars of his reflection.

A gull had wings under his
and remarked that the air
was "like marble." He said: "Up here
I tower through the sky
for the marble wings on my tower-top fly."

But he sleeps on the top of his mast
with his eyes closed tight.
The gull inquired into his dream,
which was, "I must not fall.
The spangled sea below wants me to fall.
It is hard as diamonds; it wants to destroy us all."

The Monument

Now can you see the monument? It is of wood
built somewhat like a box. No. Built
like several boxes in descending sizes
one above the other.
Each is turned half-way round so that
its corners point toward the sides
of the one below and the angles alternate.
Then on the topmost cube is set
a sort of fleur-de-lys of weathered wood,
long petals of board, pierced with odd holes,
four-sided, stiff, ecclesiastical.
From it four thin, warped poles spring out,
(slanted like fishing-poles or flag-poles)
and from them jig-saw work hangs down,
four lines of vaguely whittled ornament
over the edges of the boxes
to the ground.
The monument is one-third set against
a sea; two-thirds against a sky.
The view is geared
(that is, the view's perspective)
so low there is no "far away,"
and we are far away within the view.
A sea of narrow, horizontal boards
lies out behind our lonely monument,
its long grains alternating right and left
like floor-boards—spotted, swarming-still,
and motionless. A sky runs parallel,
and it is palings, coarser than the sea's:
splintery sunlight and long-fibred clouds.
"Why does that strange sea make no sound?
Is it because we're far away?
Where are we? Are we in Asia Minor,
Or in Mongolia?"
                    An ancient promontory,
an ancient principality whose artist-prince

25

might have wanted to build a monument
to mark a tomb or boundary, or make
a melancholy or romantic scene of it . . .
"But that queer sea looks made of wood,
half-shining, like a driftwood sea.
And the sky looks wooden, grained with cloud.
It's like a stage-set; it is all so flat!
Those clouds are full of glistening splinters!
What is that?"
                  It is the monument.
"It's piled-up boxes,
outlined with shoddy fret-work, half-fallen off,
cracked and unpainted. It looks old."
—The strong sunlight, the wind from the sea,
all the conditions of its existence,
may have flaked off the paint, if ever it was painted,
and made it homelier than it was.
"Why did you bring me here to see it?
A temple of crates in cramped and crated scenery,
what can it prove?
I am tired of breathing this eroded air,
this dryness in which the monument is cracking."

It is an artifact
of wood. Wood holds together better
than sea or cloud or sand could by itself,
much better than real sea or sand or cloud.
It chose that way to grow and not to move.
The monument's an object, yet those decorations,
carelessly nailed, looking like nothing at all,
give it away as having life, and wishing;
wanting to be a monument, to cherish something.
The crudest scroll-work says "commemorate,"
while once each day the light goes around it
like a prowling animal,
or the rain falls on it, or the wind blows into it.
It may be solid, may be hollow.
The bones of the artist-prince may be inside
or far away on even drier soil.
But roughly but adequately it can shelter

what is within (which after all
cannot have been intended to be seen).
It is the beginning of a painting,
a piece of sculpture, or poem, or monument,
and all of wood. Watch it closely.

Paris, 7 A.M.

I make a trip to each clock in the apartment:
some hands point histrionically one way
and some point others, from the ignorant faces.
Time is an Etoile; the hours diverge
so much that days are journeys round the suburbs,
circles surrounding stars, overlapping circles.
The short, half-tone scale of winter weathers
is a spread pigeon's wing.
Winter lives under a pigeon's wing, a dead wing with damp feathers.

Look down into the courtyard. All the houses
are built that way, with ornamental urns
set on the mansard roof-tops where the pigeons
take their walks. It is like introspection
to stare inside, or retrospection,
a star inside a rectangle, a recollection:
this hollow square could easily have been there.
—The childish snow-forts, built in flashier winters,
could have reached these proportions and been houses;
the mighty snow-forts, four, five, stories high,
withstanding spring as sand-forts do the tide,
their walls, their shape, could not dissolve and die,
only be overlapping in a strong chain, turned to stone,
and grayed and yellowed now like these.

Where is the ammunition, the piled-up balls
with the star-splintered hearts of ice?
This sky is no carrier-warrior-pigeon
escaping endless intersecting circles.
It is a dead one, or the sky from which a dead one fell.
The urns have caught his ashes or his feathers.
When did the star dissolve, or was it captured
by the sequence of squares and squares and circles, circles?
Can the clocks say; is it there below,
about to tumble in snow?

Quai d'Orléans

for Margaret Miller

Each barge on the river easily tows
    a mighty wake,
a giant oak-leaf of gray lights
    on duller gray;
and behind it real leaves are floating by,
    down to the sea.
Mercury-veins on the giant leaves,
    the ripples, make
for the sides of the quai, to extinguish themselves
    against the walls
as softly as falling-stars come to their ends
    at a point in the sky.
And throngs of small leaves, real leaves, trailing them,
    go drifting by
to disappear as modestly, down the sea's
    dissolving halls.
We stand as still as stones to watch
    the leaves and ripples
while light and nervous water hold
    their interview.
"If what we see could forget us half as easily,"
    I want to tell you,
"as it does itself—but for life we'll not be rid
    of the leaves' fossils."

Sleeping on the Ceiling

It is so peaceful on the ceiling!
It is the Place de la Concorde.
The little crystal chandelier
is off, the fountain is in the dark.
Not a soul is in the park.

Below, where the wallpaper is peeling,
the Jardin des Plantes has locked its gates.
Those photographs are animals.
The mighty flowers and foliage rustle;
under the leaves the insects tunnel.

We must go under the wallpaper
to meet the insect-gladiator,
to battle with a net and trident,
and leave the fountain and the square.
But oh, that we could sleep up there. . . .

Sleeping Standing Up

As we lie down to sleep the world turns half away
        through ninety dark degrees;
                the bureau lies on the wall
and thoughts that were recumbent in the day
            rise as the others fall,
        stand up and make a forest of thick-set trees.

The armored cars of dreams, contrived to let us do
        so many a dangerous thing,
                are chugging at its edge
all camouflaged, and ready to go through
            the swiftest streams, or up a ledge
        of crumbling shale, while plates and trappings ring.

—Through turret-slits we saw the crumbs or pebbles that lay
        below the riveted flanks
                on the green forest floor,
like those the clever children placed by day
            and followed to their door
        one night, at least; and in the ugly tanks

we tracked them all the night. Sometimes they disappeared,
        dissolving in the moss,
                sometimes we went too fast
and ground them underneath. How stupidly we steered
            until the night was past
        and never found out where the cottage was.

Cirque d'Hiver

Across the floor flits the mechanical toy,
fit for a king of several centuries back.
A little circus horse with real white hair.
His eyes are glossy black.
He bears a little dancer on his back.

She stands upon her toes and turns and turns.
A slanting spray of artificial roses
is stitched across her skirt and tinsel bodice.
Above her head she poses
another spray of artificial roses.

His mane and tail are straight from Chirico.
He has a formal, melancholy soul.
He feels her pink toes dangle toward his back
along the little pole
that pierces both her body and her soul

and goes through his, and reappears below,
under his belly, as a big tin key.
He canters three steps, then he makes a bow,
canters again, bows on one knee,
canters, then clicks and stops, and looks at me.

The dancer, by this time, has turned her back.
He is the more intelligent by far.
Facing each other rather desperately—
his eye is like a star—
we stare and say, "Well, we have come this far."

Florida

The state with the prettiest name,
the state that floats in brackish water,
held together by mangrove roots
that bear while living oysters in clusters,
and when dead strew white swamps with skeletons,
dotted as if bombarded, with green hummocks
like ancient cannon-balls sprouting grass.
The state full of long S-shaped birds, blue and white,
and unseen hysterical birds who rush up the scale
every time in a tantrum.
Tanagers embarrassed by their flashiness,
and pelicans whose delight it is to clown;
who coast for fun on the strong tidal currents
in and out among the mangrove islands
and stand on the sand-bars drying their damp gold wings
on sun-lit evenings.
Enormous turtles, helpless and mild,
die and leave their barnacled shells on the beaches,
and their large white skulls with round eye-sockets
twice the size of a man's.
The palm trees clatter in the stiff breeze
like the bills of the pelicans. The tropical rain comes down
to freshen the tide-looped strings of fading shells:
Job's Tear, the Chinese Alphabet, the scarce Junonia,
parti-colored pectins and Ladies' Ears,
arranged as on a gray rag of rotted calico,
the buried Indian Princess's skirt;
with these the monotonous, endless, sagging coast-line
is delicately ornamented.

Thirty or more buzzards are drifting down, down, down,
over something they have spotted in the swamp,
in circles like stirred-up flakes of sediment
sinking through water.
Smoke from woods-fires filters fine blue solvents.
On stumps and dead trees the charring is like black velvet.

The mosquitoes
go hunting to the tune of their ferocious obbligatos.
After dark, the fireflies map the heavens in the marsh
until the moon rises.
Cold white, not bright, the moonlight is coarse-meshed,
and the careless, corrupt state is all black specks
too far apart, and ugly whites; the poorest
post-card of itself.
After dark, the pools seem to have slipped away.
The alligator, who has five distinct calls:
friendliness, love, mating, war, and a warning—
whimpers and speaks in the throat
of the Indian Princess.

Jerónimo's House

My house, my fairy
    palace, is
of perishable
    clapboards with
three rooms in all,
    my gray wasps' nest
of chewed-up paper
    glued with spit.

My home, my love-nest,
    is endowed
with a veranda
    of wooden lace,
adorned with ferns
    planted in sponges,
and the front room
    with red and green

left-over Christmas
    decorations
looped from the corners
    to the middle
above my little
    center table
of woven wicker
    painted blue,

and four blue chairs
    and an affair
for the smallest baby
    with a tray
with ten big beads.
    Then on the walls
two palm-leaf fans
    and a calendar

and on the table
    one fried fish
spattered with burning
    scarlet sauce,
a little dish
    of hominy grits
and four pink tissue-
    paper roses.

Also I have
    hung on a hook,
an old French horn
    repainted with
aluminum paint.
    I play each year
in the parade
    for José Marti.

At night you'd think
    my house abandoned.
Come closer. You
    can see and hear
the writing-paper
    lines of light
and the voices of
    my radio

singing flamencos
    in between
the lottery numbers.
    When I move
I take these things,
    not much more, from
my shelter from
    the hurricane.

Roosters

At four o'clock
in the gun-metal blue dark
we hear the first crow of the first cock

just below
the gun-metal blue window
and immediately there is an echo

off in the distance,
then one from the backyard fence,
then one, with horrible insistence,

grates like a wet match
from the broccoli patch,
flares, and all over town begins to catch.

Cries galore
come from the water-closet door,
from the dropping-plastered henhouse floor,

where in the blue blur
their rustling wives admire,
the roosters brace their cruel feet and glare

with stupid eyes
while from their beaks there rise
the uncontrolled, traditional cries.

Deep from protruding chests
in green-gold medals dressed,
planned to command and terrorize the rest,

the many wives
who lead hens' lives
of being courted and despised;

deep from raw throats
a senseless order floats
all over town. A rooster gloats

over our beds
from rusty iron sheds
and fences made from old bedsteads,

over our churches
where the tin rooster perches,
over our little wooden northern houses,

making sallies
from all the muddy alleys,
marking out maps like Rand McNally's:

glass-headed pins,
oil-golds and copper greens,
anthracite blues, alizarins,

each one an active
displacement in perspective;
each screaming, "This is where I live!"

Each screaming
"Get up! Stop dreaming!"
Roosters, what are you projecting?

You, whom the Greeks elected
to shoot at on a post, who struggled
when sacrificed, you whom they labeled

"Very combative . . ."
what right have you to give
commands and tell us how to live,

cry "Here!" and "Here!"
and wake us here where are
unwanted love, conceit and war?

The crown of red
set on your little head
is charged with all your fighting blood.

Yes, that excrescence
makes a most virile presence,
plus all that vulgar beauty of iridescence.

Now in mid-air
by twos they fight each other.
Down comes a first flame-feather,

and one is flying,
with raging heroism defying
even the sensation of dying.

And one has fallen,
but still above the town
his torn-out, bloodied feathers drift down;

and what he sung
no matter. He is flung
on the gray ash-heap, lies in dung

with his dead wives
with open, bloody eyes,
while those metallic feathers oxidize.

St. Peter's sin
was worse than that of Magdalen
whose sin was of the flesh alone;

of spirit, Peter's,
falling, beneath the flares,
among the "servants and officers."

Old holy sculpture
could set it all together
in one small scene, past and future:

Christ stands amazed,
Peter, two fingers raised
to surprised lips, both as if dazed.

But in between
a little cock is seen
carved on a dim column in the travertine

explained by *gallus canit*;
flet Petrus underneath it.
There is inescapable hope, the pivot;

yes, and there Peter's tears
run down our chanticleer's
sides and gem his spurs.

Tear-encrusted thick
as a medieval relic
he waits. Poor Peter, heart-sick,

still cannot guess
those cock-a-doodles yet might bless,
his dreadful rooster come to mean forgiveness,

a new weathervane
on basilica and barn,
and that outside the Lateran

there would always be
a bronze cock on a porphyry
pillar so the people and the Pope might see

that even the Prince
of the Apostles long since
had been forgiven, and to convince

all the assembly
that "Deny deny deny"
is not all the roosters cry.

In the morning
a low light is floating
in the backyard, and gilding

from underneath
the broccoli, leaf by leaf;
how could the night have come to grief?

gilding the tiny
floating swallow's belly
and lines of pink cloud in the sky,

the day's preamble
like wandering lines in marble.
The cocks are now almost inaudible.

The sun climbs in,
following "to see the end,"
faithful as enemy, or friend.

Seascape

This celestial seascape, with white herons got up as angels,
flying as high as they want and as far as they want sidewise
in tiers and tiers of immaculate reflections;
the whole region, from the highest heron
down to the weightless mangrove island
with bright green leaves edged neatly with bird-droppings
like illumination in silver,
and down to the suggestively Gothic arches of the mangrove roots
and the beautiful pea-green back-pasture
where occasionally a fish jumps, like a wild-flower
in an ornamental spray of spray;
this cartoon by Raphael for a tapestry for a Pope:
it does look like heaven.
But a skeletal lighthouse standing there
in black and white clerical dress,
who lives on his nerves, thinks he knows better.
He thinks that hell rages below his iron feet,
that that is why the shallow water is so warm,
and he knows that heaven is not like this.
Heaven is not like flying or swimming,
but has something to do with blackness and a strong glare
and when it gets dark he will remember something
strongly worded to say on the subject.

Little Exercise

for Thomas Edwards Wanning

Think of the storm roaming the sky uneasily
like a dog looking for a place to sleep in,
listen to it growling.

Think how they must look now, the mangrove keys
lying out there unresponsive to the lightning
in dark, coarse-fibred families,

where occasionally a heron may undo his head,
shake up his feathers, make an uncertain comment
when the surrounding water shines.

Think of the boulevard and the little palm trees
all stuck in rows, suddenly revealed
as fistfuls of limp fish-skeletons.

It is raining there. The boulevard
and its broken sidewalks with weeds in every crack
are relieved to be wet, the sea to be freshened.

Now the storm goes away again in a series
of small, badly lit battle-scenes,
each in "Another part of the field."

Think of someone sleeping in the bottom of a row-boat
tied to a mangrove root or the pile of a bridge;
think of him as uninjured, barely disturbed.

The Fish

I caught a tremendous fish
and held him beside the boat
half out of water, with my hook
fast in a corner of his mouth.
He didn't fight.
He hadn't fought at all.
He hung a grunting weight,
battered and venerable
and homely. Here and there
his brown skin hung in strips
like ancient wallpaper,
and its pattern of darker brown
was like wallpaper:
shapes like full-blown roses
stained and lost through age.
He was speckled with barnacles,
fine rosettes of lime,
and infested
with tiny white sea-lice,
and underneath two or three
rags of green weed hung down.
While his gills were breathing in
the terrible oxygen
—the frightening gills,
fresh and crisp with blood,
that can cut so badly—
I thought of the coarse white flesh
packed in like feathers,
the big bones and the little bones,
the dramatic reds and blacks
of his shiny entrails,
and the pink swim-bladder
like a big peony.
I looked into his eyes
which were far larger than mine
but shallower, and yellowed,

the irises backed and packed
with tarnished tinfoil
seen through the lenses
of old scratched isinglass.
They shifted a little, but not
to return my stare.
—It was more like the tipping
of an object toward the light.
I admired his sullen face,
the mechanism of his jaw,
and then I saw
that from his lower lip
—if you could call it a lip—
grim, wet, and weaponlike,
hung five old pieces of fish-line,
or four and a wire leader
with the swivel still attached,
with all their five big hooks
grown firmly in his mouth.
A green line, frayed at the end
where he broke it, two heavier lines,
and a fine black thread
still crimped from the strain and snap
when it broke and he got away.
Like medals with their ribbons
frayed and wavering,
a five-haired beard of wisdom
trailing from his aching jaw.
I stared and stared
and victory filled up
the little rented boat,
from the pool of bilge
where oil had spread a rainbow
around the rusted engine
to the bailer rusted orange,
the sun-cracked thwarts,
the oarlocks on their strings,
the gunnels—until everything
was rainbow, rainbow, rainbow!
And I let the fish go.

Late Air

From a magician's midnight sleeve
    the radio-singers
distribute all their love-songs
over the dew-wet lawns.
    And like a fortune-teller's
their marrow-piercing guesses are whatever you believe.

But on the Navy Yard aerial I find
    better witnesses
for love on summer nights.
Five remote red lights
    keep their nests there; Phoenixes
burning quietly, where the dew cannot climb.

Cootchie

Cootchie, Miss Lula's servant, lies in marl,
black into white she went
    below the surface of the coral-reef.
Her life was spent
    in caring for Miss Lula, who is deaf,
eating her dinner off the kitchen sink
while Lula ate hers off the kitchen table.
The skies were egg-white for the funeral
    and the faces sable.

Tonight the moonlight will alleviate
the melting of the pink wax roses
    planted in tin cans filled with sand
placed in a line to mark Miss Lula's losses;
    but who will shout and make her understand?
Searching the land and sea for someone else,
the lighthouse will discover Cootchie's grave
and dismiss all as trivial; the sea, desperate,
    will proffer wave after wave.

Songs for a Colored Singer

A washing hangs upon the line,
    but it's not mine.
None of the things that I can see
    belong to me.
The neighbors got a radio with an aerial;
    we got a little portable.
They got a lot of closet space;
    we got a suitcase.

I say, "Le Roy, just how much are we owing?
Something I can't comprehend,
the more we got the more we spend. . . ."
He only answers, "Let's get going."
Le Roy, you're earning too much money now.

I sit and look at our backyard
    and find it very hard.
What have we got for all his dollars and cents?
    —A pile of bottles by the fence.
He's faithful and he's kind
    but he sure has an inquiring mind.
He's seen a lot; he's bound to see the rest,
    and if I protest

Le Roy answers with a frown,
"Darling, when I earns I spends.
The world is wide; it still extends. . . .
I'm going to get a job in the next town."
Le Roy, you're earning too much money now.

II

The time has come to call a halt;
    and so it ends.
    He's gone off with his other friends.
    He needn't try to make amends,
this occasion's all his fault.
    Through rain and dark I see his face
    across the street at Flossie's place.
    He's drinking in the warm pink glow
    to th' accompaniment of the piccolo.*

The time has come to call a halt.
I met him walking with Varella
and hit him twice with my umbrella.
Perhaps that occasion was my fault,
but the time has come to call a halt.

Go drink your wine and go get tight.
    Let the piccolo play.
    I'm sick of all your fussing anyway.
    Now I'm pursuing my own way.
I'm leaving on the bus tonight.
    Far down the highway wet and black
    I'll ride and ride and not come back.
    I'm going to go and take the bus
    and find someone monogamous.

The time has come to call a halt.
I've borrowed fifteen dollars fare
and it will take me anywhere.
For this occasion's all his fault.
The time has come to call a halt.

*Jukebox.

III

Lullaby.
Adult and child
sink to their rest.
At sea the big ship sinks and dies,
lead in its breast.

Lullaby.
Let nations rage,
let nations fall.
The shadow of the crib makes an enormous cage
upon the wall.

Lullaby.
Sleep on and on,
war's over soon.
Drop the silly, harmless toy,
pick up the moon.

Lullaby.
If they should say
you have no sense,
don't you mind them; it won't make
much difference.

Lullaby.
Adult and child
sink to their rest.
At sea the big ship sinks and dies,
lead in its breast.

IV

What's that shining in the leaves,
the shadowy leaves,
like tears when somebody grieves,
shining, shining in the leaves?

Is it dew or is it tears,
dew or tears,
hanging there for years and years
like a heavy dew of tears?

Then that dew begins to fall,
roll down and fall.
Maybe it's not tears at all.
See it, see it roll and fall.

Hear it falling on the ground,
hear, all around.
That is not a tearful sound,
beating, beating on the ground.

See it lying there like seeds,
like black seeds.
See it taking root like weeds,
faster, faster than the weeds,

all the shining seeds take root,
conspiring root,
and what curious flower or fruit
will grow from that conspiring root?

Fruit or flower? It is a face.
Yes, a face.
In that dark and dreary place
each seed grows into a face.

Like an army in a dream
the faces seem,
darker, darker, like a dream.
They're too real to be a dream.

Anaphora

in memory of Marjorie Carr Stevens

Each day with so much ceremony
begins, with birds, with bells,
with whistles from a factory;
such white-gold skies our eyes
first open on, such brilliant walls
that for a moment we wonder
"Where is the music coming from, the energy?
The day was meant for what ineffable creature
we must have missed?" Oh promptly he
appears and takes his earthly nature
    instantly, instantly falls
    victim of long intrigue,
    assuming memory and mortal
    mortal fatigue.

More slowly falling into sight
and showering into stippled faces,
darkening, condensing all his light;
in spite of all the dreaming
squandered upon him with that look,
suffers our uses and abuses,
sinks through the drift of bodies,
sinks through the drift of classes
to evening to the beggar in the park
who, weary, without lamp or book
    prepares stupendous studies:
    the fiery event
    of every day in endless
    endless assent.

A Cold Spring (1955)

TO DR. ANNY BAUMANN

A Cold Spring

for Jane Dewey, Maryland

Nothing is so beautiful as spring.   —Hopkins

A cold spring:
the violet was flawed on the lawn.
For two weeks or more the trees hesitated;
the little leaves waited,
carefully indicating their characteristics.
Finally a grave green dust
settled over your big and aimless hills.
One day, in a chill white blast of sunshine,
on the side of one a calf was born.
The mother stopped lowing
and took a long time eating the after-birth,
a wretched flag,
but the calf got up promptly
and seemed inclined to feel gay.

The next day
was much warmer.
Greenish-white dogwood infiltrated the wood,
each petal burned, apparently, by a cigarette-butt;
and the blurred redbud stood
beside it, motionless, but almost more
like movement than any placeable color.
Four deer practised leaping over your fences.
The infant oak-leaves swung through the sober oak.
Song-sparrows were wound up for the summer,
and in the maple the complementary cardinal
cracked a whip, and the sleeper awoke,
stretching miles of green limbs from the south.
In his cap the lilacs whitened,
then one day they fell like snow.
Now, in the evening,
a new moon comes.
The hills grow softer. Tufts of long grass show
Where each cow-flop lies.
The bull-frogs are sounding,
slack strings plucked by heavy thumbs.

Beneath the light, against your white front door,
the smallest moths, like Chinese fans,
flatten themselves, silver and silver-gilt
over pale yellow, orange, or gray.
Now, from the thick grass, the fireflies
begin to rise:
up, then down, then up again:
lit on the ascending flight,
drifting simultaneously to the same height,
—exactly like the bubbles in champagne.
—Later on they rise much higher.
And your shadowy pastures will be able to offer
these particular glowing tributes
every evening now throughout the summer.

Over 2,000 Illustrations and
a Complete Concordance

Thus should have been our travels:
serious, engravable.
The Seven Wonders of the World are tired
and a touch familiar, but the other scenes,
innumerable, though equally sad and still,
are foreign. Often the squatting Arab,
or group of Arabs, plotting, probably,
against our Christian Empire,
while one apart, with outstretched arm and hand
points to the Tomb, the Pit, the Sepulcher.
The branches of the date-palms look like files.
The cobbled courtyard, where the Well is dry,
is like a diagram, the brickwork conduits
are vast and obvious, the human figure
far gone in history or theology,
gone with its camel or its faithful horse.
Always the silence, the gesture, the specks of birds
suspended on invisible threads above the Site,
or the smoke rising solemnly, pulled by threads.
Granted a page alone or a page made up
of several scenes arranged in cattycornered rectangles
or circles set on stippled gray,
granted a grim lunette,
caught in the toils of an initial letter,
when dwelt upon, they all resolve themselves.
The eye drops, weighted, through the lines
the burin made, the lines that move apart
like ripples above sand,
dispersing storms, God's spreading fingerprint,
and painfully, finally, that ignite
in watery prismatic white-and-blue.

Entering the Narrows at St. Johns
the touching bleat of goats reached to the ship.
We glimpsed them, reddish, leaping up the cliffs
among the fog-soaked weeds and butter-and-eggs.

And at St. Peter's the wind blew and the sun shone madly.
Rapidly, purposefully, the Collegians marched in lines,
crisscrossing the great square with black, like ants.
In Mexico the dead man lay
in a blue arcade; the dead volcanoes
glistened like Easter lilies.
The jukebox went on playing "Ay, Jalisco!"
And at Volubilis there were beautiful poppies
splitting the mosaics; the fat old guide made eyes.
In Dingle harbor a golden length of evening
the rotting hulks held up their dripping plush.
The Englishwoman poured tea, informing us
that the Duchess was going to have a baby.
And in the brothels of Marrakesh
the little pockmarked prostitutes
balanced their tea-trays on their heads
and did their belly-dances; flung themselves
naked and giggling against our knees,
asking for cigarettes. It was somewhere near there
I saw what frightened me most of all:
A holy grave, not looking particularly holy,
one of a group under a keyhole-arched stone baldaquin
open to every wind from the pink desert.
An open, gritty, marble trough, carved solid
with exhortation, yellowed
as scattered cattle-teeth;
half-filled with dust, not even the dust
of the poor prophet paynim who once lay there.
In a smart burnoose Khadour looked on amused.

Everything only connected by "and" and "and."
Open the book. (The gilt rubs off the edges
of the pages and pollinates the fingertips.)
Open the heavy book. Why couldn't we have seen
this old Nativity while we were at it?
—the dark ajar, the rocks breaking with light,
an undisturbed, unbreathing flame,
colorless, sparkless, freely fed on straw,
and, lulled within, a family with pets,
—and looked and looked our infant sight away.

The Bight

[On my birthday]

At low tide like this how sheer the water is.
White, crumbling ribs of marl protrude and glare
and the boats are dry, the pilings dry as matches.
Absorbing, rather than being absorbed,
the water in the bight doesn't wet anything,
the color of the gas flame turned as low as possible.
One can smell it turning to gas; if one were Baudelaire
one could probably hear it turning to marimba music.
The little ocher dredge at work off the end of the dock
already plays the dry perfectly off-beat claves.
The birds are outsize. Pelicans crash
into this peculiar gas unnecessarily hard,
it seems to me, like pickaxes,
rarely coming up with anything to show for it,
and going off with humorous elbowings.
Black-and-white man-of-war birds soar
on impalpable drafts
and open their tails like scissors on the curves
or tense them like wishbones, till they tremble.
The frowsy sponge boats keep coming in
with the obliging air of retrievers,
bristling with jackstraw gaffs and hooks
and decorated with bobbles of sponges.
There is a fence of chicken wire along the dock
where, glinting like little plowshares,
the blue-gray shark tails are hung up to dry
for the Chinese-restaurant trade.
Some of the little white boats are still piled up
against each other, or lie on their sides, stove in,
and not yet salvaged, if they ever will be, from the last bad storm,
like torn-open, unanswered letters.
The bight is littered with old correspondences.
Click. Click. Goes the dredge,
and brings up a dripping jawful of marl.
All the untidy activity continues,
awful but cheerful.

A Summer's Dream

To the sagging wharf
few ships could come.
The population numbered
two giants, an idiot, a dwarf,

a gentle storekeeper
asleep behind his counter,
and our kind landlady—
the dwarf was her dressmaker.

The idiot could be beguiled
by picking blackberries,
but then threw them away.
The shrunken seamstress smiled.

By the sea, lying
blue as a mackerel,
our boarding house was streaked
as though it had been crying.

Extraordinary geraniums
crowded the front windows,
the floors glittered with
assorted linoleums.

Every night we listened
for a horned owl.
In the horned lamp flame,
the wallpaper glistened.

The giant with the stammer
was the landlady's son,
grumbling on the stairs
over an old grammar.

He was morose,
but she was cheerful.
The bedroom was cold,
the feather bed close.

We were wakened in the dark by
the somnambulist brook
nearing the sea,
still dreaming audibly.

At the Fishhouses

Although it is a cold evening,
down by one of the fishhouses
an old man sits netting,
his net, in the gloaming almost invisible
a dark purple-brown,
and his shuttle worn and polished.
The air smells so strong of codfish
it makes one's nose run and one's eyes water.
The five fishhouses have steeply peaked roofs
and narrow, cleated gangplanks slant up
to storerooms in the gables
for the wheelbarrows to be pushed up and down on.
All is silver: the heavy surface of the sea,
swelling slowly as if considering spilling over,
is opaque, but the silver of the benches,
the lobster pots, and masts, scattered
among the wild jagged rocks,
is of an apparent translucence
like the small old buildings with an emerald moss
growing on their shoreward walls.
The big fish tubs are completely lined
with layers of beautiful herring scales
and the wheelbarrows are similarly plastered
with creamy iridescent coats of mail,
with small iridescent flies crawling on them.
Up on the little slope behind the houses,
set in the sparse bright sprinkle of grass,
is an ancient wooden capstan,
cracked, with two long bleached handles
and some melancholy stains, like dried blood,
where the ironwork has rusted.
The old man accepts a Lucky Strike.
He was a friend of my grandfather.
We talk of the decline in the population
and of codfish and herring
while he waits for a herring boat to come in.

There are sequins on his vest and on his thumb.
He has scraped the scales, the principal beauty,
from unnumbered fish with that black old knife,
the blade of which is almost worn away.

Down at the water's edge, at the place
where they haul up the boats, up the long ramp
descending into the water, thin silver
tree trunks are laid horizontally
across the gray stones, down and down
at intervals of four or five feet.

Cold dark deep and absolutely clear,
element bearable to no mortal,
to fish and to seals . . . One seal particularly
I have seen here evening after evening.
He was curious about me. He was interested in music;
like me a believer in total immersion,
so I used to sing him Baptist hymns.
I also sang "A Mighty Fortress Is Our God."
He stood up in the water and regarded me
steadily, moving his head a little.
Then he would disappear, then suddenly emerge
almost in the same spot, with a sort of shrug
as if it were against his better judgment.
Cold dark deep and absolutely clear,
the clear gray icy water . . . Back, behind us,
the dignified tall firs begin.
Bluish, associating with their shadows,
a million Christmas trees stand
waiting for Christmas. The water seems suspended
above the rounded gray and blue-gray stones.
I have seen it over and over, the same sea, the same,
slightly, indifferently swinging above the stones,
icily free above the stones,
above the stones and then the world.
If you should dip your hand in,
your wrist would ache immediately,
your bones would begin to ache and your hand would burn
as if the water were a transmutation of fire
that feeds on stones and burns with a dark gray flame.
If you tasted it, it would first taste bitter,

then briny, then surely burn your tongue.
It is like what we imagine knowledge to be:
dark, salt, clear, moving, utterly free,
drawn from the cold hard mouth
of the world, derived from the rocky breasts
forever, flowing and drawn, and since
our knowledge is historical, flowing, and flown.

Cape Breton

Out on the high "bird islands," Ciboux and Hertford,
the razorbill auks and the silly-looking puffins all stand
with their backs to the mainland
in solemn, uneven lines along the cliff's brown grass-frayed edge,
while the few sheep pastured there go "Baaa, baaa."
(Sometimes, frightened by aeroplanes, they stampede
and fall over into the sea or onto the rocks.)
The silken water is weaving and weaving,
disappearing under the mist equally in all directions,
lifted and penetrated now and then
by one shag's dripping serpent-neck,
and somewhere the mist incorporates the pulse,
rapid but unurgent, of a motorboat.

The same mist hangs in thin layers
among the valleys and gorges of the mainland
like rotting snow-ice sucked away
almost to spirit; the ghosts of glaciers drift
among those folds and folds of fir: spruce and hackmatack—
dull, dead, deep peacock-colors,
each riser distinguished from the next
by an irregular nervous saw-tooth edge,
alike, but certain as a stereoscopic view.

The wild road clambers along the brink of the coast.
On it stand occasional small yellow bulldozers,
but without their drivers, because today is Sunday.
The little white churches have been dropped into the matted hills
like lost quartz arrowheads.
The road appears to have been abandoned.
Whatever the landscape had of meaning appears to have been
    abandoned,
unless the road is holding it back, in the interior,
where we cannot see,
where deep lakes are reputed to be,
and disused trails and mountains of rock

and miles of burnt forests standing in gray scratches
like the admirable scriptures made on stones by stones—
and these regions now have little to say for themselves
except in thousands of light song-sparrow songs floating upward
freely, dispassionately, through the mist, and meshing
in brown-wet, fine, torn fish-nets.

A small bus comes along, in up-and-down rushes,
packed with people, even to its step.
(On weekdays with groceries, spare automobile parts, and pump parts,
but today only two preachers extra, one carrying his frock coat on a
    hanger.)
It passes the closed roadside stand, the closed schoolhouse,
where today no flag is flying
from the rough-adzed pole topped with a white china doorknob.
It stops, and a man carrying a baby gets off,
climbs over a stile, and goes down through a small steep meadow,
which establishes its poverty in a snowfall of daisies,
to his invisible house beside the water.

The birds keep on singing, a calf bawls, the bus starts.
The thin mist follows
the white mutations of its dream;
an ancient chill is rippling the dark brooks.

View of The Capitol from
The Library of Congress

Moving from left to left, the light
is heavy on the Dome, and coarse.
One small lunette turns it aside
and blankly stares off to the side
like a big white old wall-eyed horse.

On the east steps the Air Force Band
in uniforms of Air Force blue
is playing hard and loud, but—queer—
the music doesn't quite come through.

It comes in snatches, dim then keen,
then mute, and yet there is no breeze.
The giant trees stand in between.
I think the trees must intervene,

catching the music in their leaves
like gold-dust, till each big leaf sags.
Unceasingly the little flags
feed their limp stripes into the air,
and the band's efforts vanish there.

Great shades, edge over,
give the music room.
The gathered brasses want to go
boom—boom.

Insomnia

The moon in the bureau mirror
looks out a million miles
(and perhaps with pride, at herself,
but she never, never smiles)
far and away beyond sleep, or
perhaps she's a daytime sleeper.

By the Universe deserted,
she'd tell it to go to hell,
and she'd find a body of water,
or a mirror, on which to dwell.
So wrap up care in a cobweb
and drop it down the well

into that world inverted
where left is always right,
where the shadows are really the body,
where we stay awake all night,
where the heavens are shallow as the sea
is now deep, and you love me.

The Prodigal

The brown enormous odor he lived by
was too close, with its breathing and thick hair,
for him to judge. The floor was rotten; the sty
was plastered halfway up with glass-smooth dung.
Light-lashed, self-righteous, above moving snouts,
the pigs' eyes followed him, a cheerful stare—
even to the sow that always ate her young—
till, sickening, he leaned to scratch her head.
But sometimes mornings after drinking bouts
(he hid the pints behind a two-by-four),
the sunrise glazed the barnyard mud with red;
the burning puddles seemed to reassure.
And then he thought he almost might endure
his exile yet another year or more.

But evenings the first star came to warn.
The farmer whom he worked for came at dark
to shut the cows and horses in the barn
beneath their overhanging clouds of hay,
with pitchforks, faint forked lightnings, catching light,
safe and companionable as in the Ark.
The pigs stuck out their little feet and snored.
The lantern—like the sun, going away—
laid on the mud a pacing aureole.
Carrying a bucket along a slimy board,
he felt the bats' uncertain staggering flight,
his shuddering insights, beyond his control,
touching him. But it took him a long time
finally to make his mind up to go home.

Faustina, or Rock Roses

Tended by Faustina
yes in a crazy house
upon a crazy bed,
frail, of chipped enamel,
blooming above her head
into four vaguely roselike
        flower-formations,

the white woman whispers to
herself. The floorboards sag
this way and that. The crooked
towel-covered table
bears a can of talcum
and five pasteboard boxes
        of little pills,

most half-crystallized.
The visitor sits and watches
the dew glint on the screen
and in it two glow-worms
burning a drowned green.
Meanwhile the eighty-watt bulb
        betrays us all,

discovering the concern
within our stupefaction;
lighting as well on heads
of tacks in the wallpaper,
on a paper wall-pocket,
violet-embossed, glistening
        with mica flakes.

It exposes the fine white hair,
the gown with the undershirt
showing at the neck,

the pallid palm-leaf fan
she holds but cannot wield,
her white disordered sheets
    like wilted roses.

Clutter of trophies,
chamber of bleached flags!
—Rags or ragged garments
hung on the chairs and hooks
each contributing its
shade of white, confusing
    as undazzling.

The visitor is embarrassed
not by pain nor age
nor even nakedness,
though perhaps by its reverse.
By and by the whisper
says, *"Faustina, Faustina . . ."*
    "¡Vengo, señora!"

On bare scraping feet
Faustina nears the bed.
She exhibits the talcum powder,
the pills, the cans of "cream,"
the white bowl of farina,
requesting for herself
    a little *coñac*;

complaining of, explaining,
the terms of her employment.
She bends above the other.
Her sinister kind face
presents a cruel black
coincident conundrum.
    Oh, is it

freedom at last, a lifelong
dream of time and silence,
dream of protection and rest?
Or is it the very worst,

the unimaginable nightmare
that never before dared last
      more than a second?

The acuteness of the question
forks instantly and starts
a snake-tongue flickering;
blurs further, blunts, softens,
separates, falls, our problems
becoming helplessly
      proliferative.

There is no way of telling.
The eyes say only either.
At last the visitor rises,
awkwardly proffers her bunch
of rust-perforated roses
and wonders oh, whence come
      all the petals.

Varick Street

At night the factories
struggle awake,
wretched uneasy buildings
veined with pipes
attempt their work.
Trying to breathe,
the elongated nostrils
haired with spikes
give off such stenches, too.
And I shall sell you sell you
sell you of course, my dear, and you'll sell me.

On certain floors
certain wonders.
Pale dirty light,
some captured iceberg
being prevented from melting.
See the mechanical moons,
sick, being made
to wax and wane
at somebody's instigation.
And I shall sell you sell you
sell you of course, my dear, and you'll sell me.

Lights music of love
work on. The presses
print calendars
I suppose; the moons
make medicine
or confectionery. Our bed
shrinks from the soot
and hapless odors
hold us close.
And I shall sell you sell you
sell you of course, my dear, and you'll sell me.

Four Poems

I / *Conversation*

The tumult in the heart
keeps asking questions.
And then it stops and undertakes to answer
in the same tone of voice.
No one could tell the difference.

Uninnocent, these conversations start,
and then engage the senses,
only half-meaning to.
And then there is no choice,
and then there is no sense;

until a name
and all its connotations are the same.

II / Rain Towards Morning

The great light cage has broken up in the air,
freeing, I think, about a million birds
whose wild ascending shadows will not be back,
and all the wires come falling down.
No cage, no frightening birds; the rain
is brightening now. The face is pale
that tried the puzzle of their prison
and solved it with an unexpected kiss,
whose freckled unsuspected hands alit.

III / *While Someone Telephones*

Wasted, wasted minutes that couldn't be worse,
minutes of a barbaric condescension.
—Stare out the bathroom window at the fir-trees,
at their dark needles, accretions to no purpose
woodenly crystallized, and where two fireflies
are only lost.
Hear nothing but a train that goes by, must go by, like tension;
nothing. And wait:
maybe even now these minutes' host
emerges, some relaxed uncondescending stranger,
the heart's release.
And while the fireflies
are failing to illuminate these nightmare trees
might they not be his green gay eyes.

IV / *O Breath*

Beneath that loved   and celebrated breast,
silent, bored really   blindly veined,
grieves, maybe   lives and lets
live, passes   bets,
something moving   but invisibly,
and with what clamor   why restrained
I cannot fathom   even a ripple.
(See the thin flying   of nine black hairs
four around one   five the other nipple,
flying almost intolerably   on your own breath.)
Equivocal, but what we have in common's   bound to be there,
whatever we must own   equivalents for,
something that maybe I   could bargain with
and make a separate peace   beneath
within   if never with

Letter to N.Y.

for Louise Crane

In your next letter I wish you'd say
where you are going and what you are doing;
how are the plays, and after the plays
what other pleasures you're pursuing:

taking cabs in the middle of the night,
driving as if to save your soul
where the road goes round and round the park
and the meter glares like a moral owl,

and the trees look so queer and green
standing alone in big black caves
and suddenly you're in a different place
where everything seems to happen in waves,

and most of the jokes you just can't catch,
like dirty words rubbed off a slate,
and the songs are loud but somehow dim
and it gets so terribly late,

and coming out of the brownstone house
to the gray sidewalk, the watered street,
one side of the buildings rises with the sun
like a glistening field of wheat.

—Wheat, not oats, dear. I'm afraid
if it's wheat it's none of your sowing,
nevertheless I'd like to know
what you are doing and where you are going.

Argument

Days that cannot bring you near
or will not,
Distance trying to appear
something more than obstinate,
argue argue argue with me
endlessly
neither proving you less wanted nor less dear.

Distance: Remember all that land
beneath the plane;
that coastline
of dim beaches deep in sand
stretching indistinguishably
all the way,
all the way to where my reasons end?

Days: And think
of all those cluttered instruments,
one to a fact,
canceling each other's experience;
how they were
like some hideous calendar
"Compliments of Never & Forever, Inc."

The intimidating sound
of these voices
we must separately find
can and shall be vanquished:
Days and Distance disarrayed again
and gone
both for good and from the gentle battleground.

Invitation to Miss Marianne Moore

From Brooklyn, over the Brooklyn Bridge, on this fine morning,
        please come flying.
In a cloud of fiery pale chemicals,
        please come flying,
to the rapid rolling of thousands of small blue drums
descending out of the mackerel sky
over the glittering grandstand of harbor-water,
        please come flying.

Whistles, pennants and smoke are blowing. The ships
are signaling cordially with multitudes of flags
rising and falling like birds all over the harbor.
Enter: two rivers, gracefully bearing
countless little pellucid jellies
in cut-glass epergnes dragging with silver chains.
The flight is safe; the weather is all arranged.
The waves are running in verses this fine morning.
        Please come flying.

Come with the pointed toe of each black shoe
trailing a sapphire highlight,
with a black capeful of butterfly wings and bon-mots,
with heaven knows how many angels all riding
on the broad black brim of your hat,
        please come flying.

Bearing a musical inaudible abacus,
a slight censorious frown, and blue ribbons,
        please come flying.
Facts and skyscrapers glint in the tide; Manhattan
is all awash with morals this fine morning,
        so please come flying.

Mounting the sky with natural heroism,
above the accidents, above the malignant movies,
the taxicabs and injustices at large,

while horns are resounding in your beautiful ears
that simultaneously listen to
a soft uninvented music, fit for the musk deer,
    please come flying.

For whom the grim museums will behave
like courteous male bower-birds,
for whom the agreeable lions lie in wait
on the steps of the Public Library,
eager to rise and follow through the doors
up into the reading rooms,
    please come flying.
We can sit down and weep; we can go shopping,
or play at a game of constantly being wrong
with a priceless set of vocabularies,
or we can bravely deplore, but please
    please come flying.

With dynasties of negative constructions
darkening and dying around you,
with grammar that suddenly turns and shines
like flocks of sandpipers flying,
    please come flying.

Come like a light in the white mackerel sky,
come like a daytime comet
with a long unnebulous train of words,
from Brooklyn, over the Brooklyn Bridge, on this fine morning,
    please come flying.

The Shampoo

The still explosions on the rocks,
the lichens, grow
by spreading, gray, concentric shocks.
They have arranged
to meet the rings around the moon, although
within our memories they have not changed.

And since the heavens will attend
as long on us,
you've been, dear friend,
precipitate and pragmatical;
and look what happens. For Time is
nothing if not amenable.

The shooting stars in your black hair
in bright formation
are flocking where,
so straight, so soon?
—Come, let me wash it in this big tin basin,
battered and shiny like the moon.

Questions of Travel (1965)

. . . O dar-vos quanto tenho e quanto posso,
Que quanto mais vos pago, mais vos devo.
                                        —Camões

BRAZIL

Arrival at Santos

Here is a coast; here is a harbor;
here, after a meager diet of horizon, is some scenery:
impractically shaped and—who knows?—self-pitying mountains,
sad and harsh beneath their frivolous greenery,

with a little church on top of one. And warehouses,
some of them painted a feeble pink, or blue,
and some tall, uncertain palms. Oh, tourist,
is this how this country is going to answer you

and your immodest demands for a different world,
and a better life, and complete comprehension
of both at last, and immediately,
after eighteen days of suspension?

Finish your breakfast. The tender is coming,
a strange and ancient craft, flying a strange and brilliant rag.
So that's the flag. I never saw it before.
I somehow never thought of there *being* a flag,

but of course there was, all along. And coins, I presume,
and paper money; they remain to be seen.
And gingerly now we climb down the ladder backward,
myself and a fellow passenger named Miss Breen,

descending into the midst of twenty-six freighters
waiting to be loaded with green coffee beans.
Please, boy, do be more careful with that boat hook!
Watch out! Oh! It has caught Miss Breen's

skirt! There! Miss Breen is about seventy,
a retired police lieutenant, six feet tall,
with beautiful bright blue eyes and a kind expression.
Her home, when she is at home, is in Glens Fall

s, New York. There. We are settled.
The customs officials will speak English, we hope,
and leave us our bourbon and cigarettes.
Ports are necessities, like postage stamps, or soap,

but they seldom seem to care what impression they make,
or, like this, only attempt, since it does not matter,
the unassertive colors of soap, or postage stamps—
wasting away like the former, slipping the way the latter

do when we mail the letters we wrote on the boat,
either because the glue here is very inferior
or because of the heat. We leave Santos at once;
we are driving to the interior.

January 1952

Brazil, January 1, 1502

. . . embroidered nature . . . tapestried landscape.
—*Landscape into Art,* by Sir Kenneth Clark

Januaries, Nature greets our eyes
exactly as she must have greeted theirs:
every square inch filling in with foliage—
big leaves, little leaves, and giant leaves,
blue, blue-green, and olive,
with occasional lighter veins and edges,
or a satin underleaf turned over;
monster ferns
in silver-gray relief,
and flowers, too, like giant water lilies
up in the air—up, rather, in the leaves—
purple, yellow, two yellows, pink,
rust red and greenish white;
solid but airy; fresh as if just finished
and taken off the frame.

A blue-white sky, a simple web,
backing for feathery detail:
brief arcs, a pale-green broken wheel,
a few palms, swarthy, squat, but delicate;
and perching there in profile, beaks agape,
the big symbolic birds keep quiet,
each showing only half his puffed and padded,
pure-colored or spotted breast.
Still in the foreground there is Sin:
five sooty dragons near some massy rocks.
The rocks are worked with lichens, gray moonbursts
splattered and overlapping,
threatened from underneath by moss
in lovely hell-green flames,
attacked above
by scaling-ladder vines, oblique and neat,
"one leaf yes and one leaf no" (in Portuguese).
The lizards scarcely breathe; all eyes
are on the smaller, female one, back-to,

her wicked tail straight up and over,
red as a red-hot wire.

Just so the Christians, hard as nails,
tiny as nails, and glinting,
in creaking armor, came and found it all,
not unfamiliar:
no lovers' walks, no bowers,
no cherries to be picked, no lute music,
but corresponding, nevertheless,
to an old dream of wealth and luxury
already out of style when they left home—
wealth, plus a brand-new pleasure.
Directly after Mass, humming perhaps
L'Homme armé or some such tune,
they ripped away into the hanging fabric,
each out to catch an Indian for himself—
those maddening little women who kept calling,
calling to each other (or had the birds waked up?)
and retreating, always retreating, behind it.

Questions of Travel

There are too many waterfalls here; the crowded streams
hurry too rapidly down to the sea,
and the pressure of so many clouds on the mountaintops
makes them spill over the sides in soft slow-motion,
turning to waterfalls under our very eyes.
—For if those streaks, those mile-long, shiny, tearstains,
aren't waterfalls yet,
in a quick age or so, as ages go here,
they probably will be.
But if the streams and clouds keep travelling, travelling,
the mountains look like the hulls of capsized ships,
slime-hung and barnacled.

Think of the long trip home.
Should we have stayed at home and thought of here?
Where should we be today?
Is it right to be watching strangers in a play
in this strangest of theatres?
What childishness is it that while there's a breath of life
in our bodies, we are determined to rush
to see the sun the other way around?
The tiniest green hummingbird in the world?
To stare at some inexplicable old stonework,
inexplicable and impenetrable,
at any view,
instantly seen and always, always delightful?
Oh, must we dream our dreams
and have them, too?
And have we room
for one more folded sunset, still quite warm?

But surely it would have been a pity
not to have seen the trees along this road,
really exaggerated in their beauty,
not to have seen them gesturing
like noble pantomimists, robed in pink.

—Not to have had to stop for gas and heard
the sad, two-noted, wooden tune
of disparate wooden clogs
carelessly clacking over
a grease-stained filling-station floor.
(In another country the clogs would all be tested.
Each pair there would have identical pitch.)
—A pity not to have heard
the other, less primitive music of the fat brown bird
who sings above the broken gasoline pump
in a bamboo church of Jesuit baroque:
three towers, five silver crosses.
—Yes, a pity not to have pondered,
blurr'dly and inconclusively,
on what connection can exist for centuries
between the crudest wooden footwear
and, careful and finicky,
the whittled fantasies of wooden cages.
—Never to have studied history in
the weak calligraphy of songbirds' cages.
—And never to have had to listen to rain
so much like politicians' speeches:
two hours of unrelenting oratory
and then a sudden golden silence
in which the traveller takes a notebook, writes:

"Is it lack of imagination that makes us come
to imagined places, not just stay at home?
Or could Pascal have been not entirely right
about just sitting quietly in one's room?

Continent, city, country, society:
the choice is never wide and never free.
And here, or there . . . No. Should we have stayed at home,
wherever that may be?"

Squatter's Children

On the unbreathing sides of hills
they play, a specklike girl and boy,
alone, but near a specklike house.
The sun's suspended eye
blinks casually, and then they wade
gigantic waves of light and shade.
A dancing yellow spot, a pup,
attends them. Clouds are piling up;

a storm piles up behind the house.
The children play at digging holes.
The ground is hard; they try to use
one of their father's tools,
a mattock with a broken haft
the two of them can scarcely lift.
It drops and clangs. Their laughter spreads
effulgence in the thunderheads,

weak flashes of inquiry
direct as is the puppy's bark.
But to their little, soluble,
unwarrantable ark,
apparently the rain's reply
consists of echolalia,
and Mother's voice, ugly as sin,
keeps calling to them to come in.

Children, the threshold of the storm
has slid beneath your muddy shoes;
wet and beguiled, you stand among
the mansions you may choose
out of a bigger house than yours,
whose lawfulness endures.
Its soggy documents retain
your rights in rooms of falling rain.

Manuelzinho

[Brazil. A friend of the writer is speaking.]

Half squatter, half tenant (no rent)—
a sort of inheritance; white,
in your thirties now, and supposed
to supply me with vegetables,
but you don't; or you won't; or you can't
get the idea through your brain—
the world's worst gardener since Cain.
Tilted above me, your gardens
ravish my eyes. You edge
the beds of silver cabbages
with red carnations, and lettuces
mix with alyssum. And then
umbrella ants arrive,
or it rains for a solid week
and the whole thing's ruined again
and I buy you more pounds of seeds,
imported, guaranteed,
and eventually you bring me
a mystic three-legged carrot,
or a pumpkin "bigger than the baby."

I watch you through the rain,
trotting, light, on bare feet,
up the steep paths you have made—
or your father and grandfather made—
all over my property,
with your head and back inside
a sodden burlap bag,
and feel I can't endure it
another minute; then,
indoors, beside the stove,
keep on reading a book.

You steal my telephone wires,
or someone does. You starve
your horse and yourself

94

and your dogs and family.
Among endless variety,
you eat boiled cabbage stalks.
And once I yelled at you
so loud to hurry up
and fetch me those potatoes
your holey hat flew off,
you jumped out of your clogs,
leaving three objects arranged
in a triangle at my feet,
as if you'd been a gardener
in a fairy tale all this time
and at the word "potatoes"
had vanished to take up your work
of fairy prince somewhere.

The strangest things happen, to you.
Your cow eats a "poison grass"
and drops dead on the spot.
Nobody else's does.
And then your father dies,
a superior old man
with a black plush hat, and a moustache
like a white spread-eagled sea gull.
The family gathers, but you,
no, you "don't think he's dead!
I look at him. He's cold.
They're burying him today.
But you know, I don't think he's *dead*."
I give you money for the funeral
and you go and hire a *bus*
for the delighted mourners,
so I have to hand over some more
and then have to hear you tell me
you pray for me every night!

And then you come again,
sniffing and shivering,
hat in hand, with that wistful
face, like a child's fistful
of bluets or white violets,
improvident as the dawn,

and once more I provide
for a shot of penicillin
down at the pharmacy, or
one more bottle of
Electrical Baby Syrup.
Or, briskly, you come to settle
what we call our "accounts,"
with two old copybooks,
one with flowers on the cover,
the other with a camel.
Immediate confusion.
You've left out the decimal points.
Your columns stagger,
honeycombed with zeros.
You whisper conspiratorially;
the numbers mount to millions.
Account books? They are Dream Books.
In the kitchen we dream together
how the meek shall inherit the earth—
or several acres of mine.

With blue sugar bags on their heads,
carrying your lunch,
your children scuttle by me
like little moles aboveground,
or even crouch behind bushes
as if I were out to shoot them!
—Impossible to make friends,
though each will grab at once
for an orange or a piece of candy.

Twined in wisps of fog,
I see you all up there
along with Formoso, the donkey,
who brays like a pump gone dry,
then suddenly stops.
—All just standing, staring
off into fog and space.
Or coming down at night,
in silence, except for hoofs,
in dim moonlight, the horse
or Formoso stumbling after.

Between us float a few
big, soft, pale-blue,
sluggish fireflies,
the jellyfish of the air . . .

Patch upon patch upon patch,
your wife keeps all of you covered.
She has gone over and over
(forearmed is forewarned)
your pair of bright-blue pants
with white thread, and these days
your limbs are draped in blueprints.
You paint—heaven knows why—
the outside of the crown
and brim of your straw hat.
Perhaps to reflect the sun?
Or perhaps when you were small,
your mother said, "Manuelzinho,
one thing: be sure you always
paint your straw hat."
One was gold for a while,
but the gold wore off, like plate.
One was bright green. Unkindly,
I called you Klorophyll Kid.
My visitors thought it was funny.
I apologize here and now.

You helpless, foolish man,
I love you all I can,
I think. Or do I?
I take off my hat, unpainted
and figurative, to you.
Again I promise to try.

Electrical Storm

Dawn an unsympathetic yellow.
Cra-aack!—dry and light.
The house was really struck.
Crack! A tinny sound, like a dropped tumbler.
Tobias jumped in the window, got in bed—
silent, his eyes bleached white, his fur on end.
Personal and spiteful as a neighbor's child,
thunder began to bang and bump the roof.
One pink flash;
then hail, the biggest size of artificial pearls.
Dead-white, wax-white, cold—
diplomats' wives' favors
from an old moon party—
they lay in melting windrows
on the red ground until well after sunrise.
We got up to find the wiring fused,
no lights, a smell of saltpetre,
and the telephone dead.

The cat stayed in the warm sheets.
The Lent trees had shed all their petals:
wet, stuck, purple, among the dead-eye pearls.

Song for the Rainy Season

Hidden, oh hidden
in the high fog
the house we live in,
beneath the magnetic rock,
rain-, rainbow-ridden,
where blood-black
bromelias, lichens,
owls, and the lint
of the waterfalls cling,
familiar, unbidden.

In a dim age
of water
the brook sings loud
from a rib cage
of giant fern; vapor
climbs up the thick growth
effortlessly, turns back,
holding them both,
house and rock,
in a private cloud.

At night, on the roof,
blind drops crawl
and the ordinary brown
owl gives us proof
he can count:
five times—always five—
he stamps and takes off
after the fat frogs that,
shrilling for love,
clamber and mount.

House, open house
to the white dew
and the milk-white sunrise

kind to the eyes,
to membership
of silver fish, mouse,
bookworms,
big moths; with a wall
for the mildew's
ignorant map;

darkened and tarnished
by the warm touch
of the warm breath,
maculate, cherished,
rejoice! For a later
era will differ.
(O difference that kills,
or intimidates, much
of all our small shadowy
life!) Without water

the great rock will stare
unmagnetized, bare,
no longer wearing
rainbows or rain,
the forgiving air
and the high fog gone;
the owls will move on
and the several
waterfalls shrivel
in the steady sun.

Sítio da Alcobaçinha
Fazenda Samambaia
Petrópolis

The Armadillo

for Robert Lowell

This is the time of year
when almost every night
the frail, illegal fire balloons appear.
Climbing the mountain height,

rising toward a saint
still honored in these parts,
the paper chambers flush and fill with light
that comes and goes, like hearts.

Once up against the sky it's hard
to tell them from the stars—
planets, that is—the tinted ones:
Venus going down, or Mars,

or the pale green one. With a wind,
they flare and falter, wobble and toss;
but if it's still they steer between
the kite sticks of the Southern Cross,

receding, dwindling, solemnly
and steadily forsaking us,
or, in the downdraft from a peak,
suddenly turning dangerous.

Last night another big one fell.
It splattered like an egg of fire
against the cliff behind the house.
The flame ran down. We saw the pair

of owls who nest there flying up
and up, their whirling black-and-white
stained bright pink underneath, until
they shrieked up out of sight.

IOI

The ancient owls' nest must have burned.
Hastily, all alone,
a glistening armadillo left the scene,
rose-flecked, head down, tail down,

and then a baby rabbit jumped out,
short-eared, to our surprise.
So soft!—a handful of intangible ash
with fixed, ignited eyes.

Too pretty, dreamlike mimicry!
O falling fire and piercing cry
and panic, and a weak mailed fist
clenched ignorant against the sky!

The Riverman

[A man in a remote Amazonian village decides to become a *sacaca*, a witch doctor who works with water spirits. The river dolphin is believed to have supernatural powers; Luandinha is a river spirit associated with the moon; and the *pirarucú* is a fish weighing up to four hundred pounds. These and other details on which this poem is based are from *Amazon Town*, by Charles Wagley.]

I got up in the night
for the Dolphin spoke to me.
He grunted beneath my window,
hid by the river mist,
but I glimpsed him—a man like myself.
I threw off my blanket, sweating;
I even tore off my shirt.
I got out of my hammock
and went through the window naked.
My wife slept and snored.
Hearing the Dolphin ahead,
I went down to the river
and the moon was burning bright
as the gasoline-lamp mantle
with the flame turned up too high,
just before it begins to scorch.
I went down to the river.
I heard the Dolphin sigh
as he slid into the water.
I stood there listening
till he called from far outstream.
I waded into the river
and suddenly a door
in the water opened inward,
groaning a little, with water
bulging above the lintel.
I looked back at my house,
white as a piece of washing
forgotten on the bank,
and I thought once of my wife,
but I knew what I was doing.

They gave me a shell of *cachaça*
and decorated cigars.
The smoke rose like mist
through the water, and our breaths
didn't make any bubbles.
We drank *cachaça* and smoked
the green cheroots. The room
filled with gray-green smoke
and my head couldn't have been dizzier.
Then a tall, beautiful serpent
in elegant white satin,
with her big eyes green and gold
like the lights on the river steamers—
yes, Luandinha, none other—
entered and greeted me.
She complimented me
in a language I didn't know;
but when she blew cigar smoke
into my ears and nostrils
I understood, like a dog,
although I can't speak it yet.
They showed me room after room
and took me from here to Belém
and back again in a minute.
In fact, I'm not sure where I went,
but miles, under the river.

Three times now I've been there.
I don't eat fish any more.
There is fine mud on my scalp
and I know from smelling my comb
that the river smells in my hair.
My hands and feet are cold.
I look yellow, my wife says,
and she brews me stinking teas
I throw out, behind her back.
Every moonlit night
I'm to go back again.
I know some things already,
but it will take years of study,
it is all so difficult.

They gave me a mottled rattle
and a pale-green coral twig
and some special weeds like smoke.
(They're under my canoe.)
When the moon shines on the river,
oh, faster than you can think it
we travel upstream and downstream,
we journey from here to there,
under the floating canoes,
right through the wicker traps,
when the moon shines on the river
and Luandinha gives a party.
Three times now I've attended.
Her rooms shine like silver
with the light from overhead,
a steady stream of light
like at the cinema.

I need a virgin mirror
no one's ever looked at,
that's never looked back at anyone,
to flash up the spirits' eyes
and help me recognize them.
The storekeeper offered me
a box of little mirrors,
but each time I picked one up
a neighbor looked over my shoulder
and then that one was spoiled—
spoiled, that is, for anything
but the girls to look at their mouths in,
to examine their teeth and smiles.

Why shouldn't I be ambitious?
I sincerely desire to be
a serious *sacaca*
like Fortunato Pombo,
or Lúcio, or even
the great Joaquim Sacaca.
Look, it stands to reason
that everything we need
can be obtained from the river.

It drains the jungles; it draws
from trees and plants and rocks
from half around the world,
it draws from the very heart
of the earth the remedy
for each of the diseases—
one just has to know how to find it.
But everything must be there
in that magic mud, beneath
the multitudes of fish,
deadly or innocent,
the giant *pirarucús*,
the turtles and crocodiles,
tree trunks and sunk canoes,
with the crayfish, with the worms
with tiny electric eyes
turning on and off and on.
The river breathes in salt
and breathes it out again,
and all is sweetness there
in the deep, enchanted silt.

When the moon burns white
and the river makes that sound
like a primus pumped up high—
that fast, high whispering
like a hundred people at once—
I'll be there below,
as the turtle rattle hisses
and the coral gives the sign,
travelling fast as a wish,
with my magic cloak of fish
swerving as I swerve,
following the veins,
the river's long, long veins,
to find the pure elixirs.
Godfathers and cousins,
your canoes are over my head;
I hear your voices talking.
You can peer down and down
or dredge the river bottom

but never, never catch me.
When the moon shines and the river
lies across the earth
and sucks it like a child,
then I will go to work
to get you health and money.
The Dolphin singled me out;
Luandinha seconded it.

Twelfth Morning; or What You Will

Like a first coat of whitewash when it's wet,
the thin gray mist lets everything show through:
the black boy Balthazár, a fence, a horse,
    a foundered house,

—cement and rafters sticking from a dune.
(The Company passes off these white but shopworn
dunes as lawns.) "Shipwreck," we say; perhaps
    this is a housewreck.

The sea's off somewhere, doing nothing. Listen.
An expelled breath. And faint, faint, faint
(or are you hearing things), the sandpipers'
    heart-broken cries.

The fence, three-strand, barbed-wire, all pure rust,
three dotted lines, comes forward hopefully
across the lots; thinks better of it; turns
    a sort of corner . . .

Don't ask the big white horse, *Are you supposed*
to be inside the fence or out? He's still
asleep. Even awake, he probably
    remains in doubt.

He's bigger than the house. The force of
personality, or is perspective dozing?
A pewter-colored horse, an ancient mixture,
    tin, lead, and silver,

he gleams a bit. But the four-gallon can
approaching on the head of Balthazár
keeps flashing that the world's a pearl, *and I*
    I am

its highlight! You can hear the water now,
inside, slap-slapping. Balthazár is singing.
"Today's my Anniversary," he sings,
    "the Day of Kings."

Cabo Frio

The Burglar of Babylon

On the fair green hills of Rio
  There grows a fearful stain:
The poor who come to Rio
  And can't go home again.

On the hills a million people,
  A million sparrows, nest,
Like a confused migration
  That's had to light and rest,

Building its nests, or houses,
  Out of nothing at all, or air.
You'd think a breath would end them,
  They perch so lightly there.

But they cling and spread like lichen,
  And the people come and come.
There's one hill called the Chicken,
  And one called Catacomb;

There's the hill of Kerosene,
  And the hill of the Skeleton,
The hill of Astonishment,
  And the hill of Babylon.

Micuçú* was a burglar and killer,
  An enemy of society.
He had escaped three times
  From the worst penitentiary.

They don't know how many he murdered
  (Though they say he never raped),

*Micuçú (mē-coo-soo) is the folk name of a deadly snake, in the north.

And he wounded two policemen
    This last time he escaped.

They said, "He'll go to his auntie,
    Who raised him like a son.
She has a little drink shop
    On the hill of Babylon."

He did go straight to his auntie,
    And he drank a final beer.
He told her, "The soldiers are coming,
    And I've got to disappear.

"Ninety years they gave me.
    Who wants to live that long?
I'll settle for ninety hours,
    On the hill of Babylon.

"Don't tell anyone you saw me.
    I'll run as long as I can.
You were good to me, and I love you,
    But I'm a doomed man."

Going out, he met a *mulata*
    Carrying water on her head.
"If you say you saw me, daughter,
    You're just as good as dead."

There are caves up there, and hideouts,
    And an old fort, falling down.
They used to watch for Frenchmen
    From the hill of Babylon.

Below him was the ocean.
    It reached far up the sky,
Flat as a wall, and on it
    Were freighters passing by,

Or climbing the wall, and climbing
    Till each looked like a fly,
And then fell over and vanished;
    And he knew he was going to die.

He could hear the goats *baa-baa*-ing,
    He could hear the babies cry;
Fluttering kites strained upward;
    And he knew he was going to die.

A buzzard flapped so near him
    He could see its naked neck.
He waved his arms and shouted,
    "Not yet, my son, not yet!"

An Army helicopter
    Came nosing around and in.
He could see two men inside it,
    But they never spotted him.

The soldiers were all over,
    On all sides of the hill,
And right against the skyline
    A row of them, small and still.

Children peeked out of windows,
    And men in the drink shop swore,
And spat a little *cachaça*
    At the light cracks in the floor.

But the soldiers were nervous, even
    With tommy guns in hand,
And one of them, in a panic,
    Shot the officer in command.

He hit him in three places;
    The other shots went wild.
The soldier had hysterics
    And sobbed like a little child.

The dying man said, "Finish
    The job we came here for."
He committed his soul to God
    And his sons to the Governor.

They ran and got a priest,
    And he died in hope of Heaven

—A man from Pernambuco,
    The youngest of eleven.

They wanted to stop the search,
    But the Army said, "No, go on,"
So the soldiers swarmed again
    Up the hill of Babylon.

Rich people in apartments
    Watched through binoculars
As long as the daylight lasted.
    And all night, under the stars,

Micuçú hid in the grasses
    Or sat in a little tree,
Listening for sounds, and staring
    At the lighthouse out at sea.

And the lighthouse stared back at him,
    Till finally it was dawn.
He was soaked with dew, and hungry,
    On the hill of Babylon.

The yellow sun was ugly,
    Like a raw egg on a plate—
Slick from the sea. He cursed it,
    For he knew it sealed his fate.

He saw the long white beaches
    And people going to swim,
With towels and beach umbrellas,
    But the soldiers were after him.

Far, far below, the people
    Were little colored spots,
And the heads of those in swimming
    Were floating coconuts.

He heard the peanut vendor
    Go *peep-peep* on his whistle,
And the man that sells umbrellas
    Swinging his watchman's rattle.

Women with market baskets
    Stood on the corners and talked,
Then went on their way to market,
    Gazing up as they walked.

The rich with their binoculars
    Were back again, and many
Were standing on the rooftops,
    Among TV antennae.

It was early, eight or eight-thirty.
    He saw a soldier climb,
Looking right at him. He fired,
    And missed for the last time.

He could hear the soldier panting,
    Though he never got very near.
Micuçú dashed for shelter.
    But he got it, behind the ear.

He heard the babies crying
    Far, far away in his head,
And the mongrels barking and barking.
    Then Micuçú was dead.

He had a Taurus revolver,
    And just the clothes he had on,
With two contos in the pockets,
    On the hill of Babylon.

The police and the populace
    Heaved a sigh of relief,
But behind the counter his auntie
    Wiped her eyes in grief.

"We have always been respected.
    My shop is honest and clean.
I loved him, but from a baby
    Micuçú was always mean.

"We have always been respected.
    His sister has a job.

Both of us gave him money.
    Why did he have to rob?

"I raised him to be honest,
    Even here, in Babylon slum."
The customers had another,
    Looking serious and glum.

But one of them said to another,
    When he got outside the door,
"He wasn't much of a burglar,
    He got caught six times—or more."

This morning the little soldiers
    Are on Babylon hill again;
Their gun barrels and helmets
    Shine in a gentle rain.

Micuçú is buried already.
    They're after another two,
But they say they aren't as dangerous
    As the poor Micuçú.

On the fair green hills of Rio
    There grows a fearful stain:
The poor who come to Rio
    And can't go home again.

There's the hill of Kerosene,
    And the hill of the Skeleton,
The hill of Astonishment,
    And the hill of Babylon.

ELSEWHERE

Manners

for a Child of 1918

My grandfather said to me
as we sat on the wagon seat,
"Be sure to remember to always
speak to everyone you meet."

We met a stranger on foot.
My grandfather's whip tapped his hat.
"Good day, sir. Good day. A fine day."
And I said it and bowed where I sat.

Then we overtook a boy we knew
with his big pet crow on his shoulder.
"Always offer everyone a ride;
don't forget that when you get older,"

my grandfather said. So Willy
climbed up with us, but the crow
gave a "Caw!" and flew off. I was worried.
How would he know where to go?

But he flew a little way at a time
from fence post to fence post, ahead;
and when Willy whistled he answered.
"A fine bird," my grandfather said,

"and he's well brought up. See, he answers
nicely when he's spoken to.
Man or beast, that's good manners.
Be sure that you both always do."

When automobiles went by,
the dust hid the people's faces,
but we shouted "Good day! Good day!
Fine day!" at the top of our voices.

When we came to Hustler Hill,
he said that the mare was tired,
so we all got down and walked,
as our good manners required.

Sestina

September rain falls on the house.
In the failing light, the old grandmother
sits in the kitchen with the child
beside the Little Marvel Stove,
reading the jokes from the almanac,
laughing and talking to hide her tears.

She thinks that her equinoctial tears
and the rain that beats on the roof of the house
were both foretold by the almanac,
but only known to a grandmother.
The iron kettle sings on the stove.
She cuts some bread and says to the child,

It's time for tea now; but the child
is watching the teakettle's small hard tears
dance like mad on the hot black stove,
the way the rain must dance on the house.
Tidying up, the old grandmother
hangs up the clever almanac

on its string. Birdlike, the almanac
hovers half open above the child,
hovers above the old grandmother
and her teacup full of dark brown tears.
She shivers and says she thinks the house
feels chilly, and puts more wood in the stove.

It was to be, says the Marvel Stove.
I know what I know, says the almanac.
With crayons the child draws a rigid house
and a winding pathway. Then the child
puts in a man with buttons like tears
and shows it proudly to the grandmother.

But secretly, while the grandmother
busies herself about the stove,
the little moons fall down like tears
from between the pages of the almanac
into the flower bed the child
has carefully placed in the front of the house.

Time to plant tears, says the almanac.
The grandmother sings to the marvellous stove
and the child draws another inscrutable house.

First Death in Nova Scotia

In the cold, cold parlor
my mother laid out Arthur
beneath the chromographs:
Edward, Prince of Wales,
with Princess Alexandra,
and King George with Queen Mary.
Below them on the table
stood a stuffed loon
shot and stuffed by Uncle
Arthur, Arthur's father.

Since Uncle Arthur fired
a bullet into him,
he hadn't said a word.
He kept his own counsel
on his white, frozen lake,
the marble-topped table.
His breast was deep and white,
cold and caressable;
his eyes were red glass,
much to be desired.

"Come," said my mother,
"Come and say good-bye
to your little cousin Arthur."
I was lifted up and given
one lily of the valley
to put in Arthur's hand.
Arthur's coffin was
a little frosted cake,
and the red-eyed loon eyed it
from his white, frozen lake.

Arthur was very small.
He was all white, like a doll
that hadn't been painted yet.

Jack Frost had started to paint him
the way he always painted
the Maple Leaf (Forever).
He had just begun on his hair,
a few red strokes, and then
Jack Frost had dropped the brush
and left him white, forever.

The gracious royal couples
were warm in red and ermine;
their feet were well wrapped up
in the ladies' ermine trains.
They invited Arthur to be
the smallest page at court.
But how could Arthur go,
clutching his tiny lily,
with his eyes shut up so tight
and the roads deep in snow?

Filling Station

Personality.

Oh, but it is dirty!
—this little filling station,
oil-soaked, oil-permeated
to a disturbing, over-all
black translucency.
Be careful with that match! *— humor?*

familiarity?

Father wears a dirty,
oil-soaked monkey suit
that cuts him under the arms,
and several quick and saucy
and greasy sons assist him *→ energy*
(it's a family filling station),
all quite thoroughly dirty.

Do they live in the station?
It has a cement porch
behind the pumps, and on it
a set of crushed and grease- *— blegh*
impregnated wickerwork;
on the wicker sofa
a dirty dog, quite comfy. *— off ent.*

Some comic books provide
the only note of color—
of certain color. They lie
upon a big dim doily
draping a taboret
(part of the set), beside
a big hirsute begonia.

Why the extraneous plant?
Why the taboret?   *viewer*
Why, oh why, the doily?   *Character?*
(Embroidered in daisy stitch

with marguerites, I think,
and heavy with gray crochet.)

Somebody embroidered the doily.
Somebody waters the plant,
or oils it, maybe. Somebody
arranges the rows of cans
so that they softly say:
ESSO—SO—SO—SO
to high-strung automobiles.
Somebody loves us all.

[handwritten annotation:] who else is there? wife/mother/sister?

Sunday, 4 A.M.

An endless and flooded
dreamland, lying low,
cross- and wheel-studded
like a tick-tack-toe.

At the right, ancillary,
"Mary" 's close and blue.
Which Mary? Aunt Mary?
Tall Mary Stearns I knew?

The old kitchen knife box,
full of rusty nails,
is at the left. A high *vox
humana* somewhere wails:

*The gray horse needs shoeing!
It's always the same!
What are you doing,
there, beyond the frame?*

*If you're the donor,
you might do that much!*
Turn on the light. Turn over.
On the bed a smutch—

black-and-gold gesso
on the altered cloth.
The cat jumps to the window;
in his mouth's a moth.

Dream dream confronting,
now the cupboard's bare.
The cat's gone a-hunting.
The brook feels for the stair.

The world seldom changes,
but the wet foot dangles
until a bird arranges
two notes at right angles.

Sandpiper

The roaring alongside he takes for granted,
and that every so often the world is bound to shake.
He runs, he runs to the south, finical, awkward,
in a state of controlled panic, a student of Blake.

The beach hisses like fat. On his left, a sheet
of interrupting water comes and goes
and glazes over his dark and brittle feet.
He runs, he runs straight through it, watching his toes.

—Watching, rather, the spaces of sand between them,
where (no detail too small) the Atlantic drains
rapidly backwards and downwards. As he runs,
he stares at the dragging grains.

The world is a mist. And then the world is
minute and vast and clear. The tide
is higher or lower. He couldn't tell you which.
His beak is focussed; he is preoccupied,

looking for something, something, something.
Poor bird, he is obsessed!
The millions of grains are black, white, tan, and gray,
mixed with quartz grains, rose and amethyst.

From Trollope's Journal

[Winter, 1861]

As far as statues go, so far there's not
much choice: they're either Washingtons
or Indians, a whitewashed, stubby lot,
His country's Father or His foster sons.
The White House in a sad, unhealthy spot
just higher than Potomac's swampy brim,
—they say the present President has got
ague or fever in each backwoods limb.
On Sunday afternoon I wandered—rather,
I floundered—out alone. The air was raw
and dark; the marsh half-ice, half-mud. This weather
is normal now: a frost, and then a thaw,
and then a frost. A hunting man, I found
the Pennsylvania Avenue heavy ground . . .
There all around me in the ugly mud
—hoof-pocked, uncultivated—herds of cattle,
numberless, wond'ring steers and oxen, stood:
beef for the Army, after the next battle.
Their legs were caked the color of dried blood;
their horns were wreathed with fog. Poor, starving, dumb
or lowing creatures, never to chew the cud
or fill their maws again! Th'effluvium
made that damned anthrax on my forehead throb.
I called a surgeon in, a young man, but,
with a sore throat himself, he did his job.
We talked about the War, and as he cut
away, he croaked out, "Sir, I do declare
everyone's sick! The soldiers poison the air."

Visits to St. Elizabeths

[1950]

This is the house of Bedlam.

This is the man
that lies in the house of Bedlam.

This is the time
of the tragic man
that lies in the house of Bedlam.

This is a wristwatch
telling the time
of the talkative man
that lies in the house of Bedlam.

This is a sailor
wearing the watch
that tells the time
of the honored man
that lies in the house of Bedlam.

This is the roadstead all of board
reached by the sailor
wearing the watch
that tells the time
of the old, brave man
that lies in the house of Bedlam.

These are the years and the walls of the ward,
the winds and clouds of the sea of board
sailed by the sailor
wearing the watch
that tells the time
of the cranky man
that lies in the house of Bedlam.

This is a Jew in a newspaper hat
that dances weeping down the ward
over the creaking sea of board
beyond the sailor
winding his watch
that tells the time
of the cruel man
that lies in the house of Bedlam.

This is a world of books gone flat.
This is a Jew in a newspaper hat
that dances weeping down the ward
over the creaking sea of board
of the batty sailor
that winds his watch
that tells the time
of the busy man
that lies in the house of Bedlam.

This is a boy that pats the floor
to see if the world is there, is flat,
for the widowed Jew in the newspaper hat
that dances weeping down the ward
waltzing the length of a weaving board
by the silent sailor
that hears his watch
that ticks the time
of the tedious man
that lies in the house of Bedlam.

These are the years and the walls and the door
that shut on a boy that pats the floor
to feel if the world is there and flat.
This is a Jew in a newspaper hat
that dances joyfully down the ward
into the parting seas of board
past the staring sailor
that shakes his watch
that tells the time
of the poet, the man
that lies in the house of Bedlam.

This is the soldier home from the war.
These are the years and the walls and the door
that shut on a boy that pats the floor
to see if the world is round or flat.
This is a Jew in a newspaper hat
that dances carefully down the ward,
walking the plank of a coffin board
with the crazy sailor
that shows his watch
that tells the time
of the wretched man
that lies in the house of Bedlam.

Translations from the Portuguese (1969)

Seven-Sided Poem

(*Carlos Drummond de Andrade*)

When I was born, one of the crooked
angels who live in shadow, said:
Carlos, go on! Be *gauche* in life.

The houses watch the men,
men who run after women.
If the afternoon had been blue,
there might have been less desire.

The trolley goes by full of legs:
white legs, black legs, yellow legs.
My God, why all the legs?
my heart asks. But my eyes
ask nothing at all.

The man behind the moustache
is serious, simple, and strong.
He hardly ever speaks.
He has a few, choice friends,
the man behind the spectacles and the moustache.

My God, why hast Thou forsaken me
if Thou knew'st I was not God,
if Thou knew'st that I was weak?

Universe, vast universe,
if I had been named Eugene
that would not be what I mean
but it would go into verse
faster.

Universe, vast universe,
my heart is vaster.*

I oughtn't to tell you,
but this moon
and this brandy
play the devil with one's emotions.

*Mundo mundo vasto mundo,
 se eu me chamasse Raimundo
 seria uma rima, não seria uma solução.
 Mundo mundo vasto mundo,
 mais vasto é meu coração.

Don't Kill Yourself

(*Carlos Drummond de Andrade*)

Carlos, keep calm, love
is what you're seeing now:
today a kiss, tomorrow no kiss,
day after tomorrow's Sunday
and nobody knows what will happen
Monday.

It's useless to resist
or to commit suicide.
Don't kill yourself. Don't kill yourself!
Keep all of yourself for the nuptials
coming nobody knows when,
that is, if they ever come.

Love, Carlos, tellurian,
spent the night with you,
and now your insides are raising
an ineffable racket,
prayers,
victrolas,
saints crossing themselves,
ads for a better soap,
a racket of which nobody
knows the why or wherefore.

In the meantime you go on your way
vertical, melancholy.
You're the palm tree, you're the cry
nobody heard in the theatre
and all the lights went out.
Love in the dark, no, love
in the daylight, is always sad,
sad, Carlos, my boy,
but tell it to nobody,
nobody knows nor shall know.

Travelling in the Family

(*Carlos Drummond de Andrade*)

to Rodrigo M. F. de Andrade

In the desert of Itabira
the shadow of my father
took me by the hand.
So much time lost.
But he didn't say anything.
It was neither day nor night.
A sigh? A passing bird?
But he didn't say anything.

We have come a long way.
Here there was a house.
The mountain used to be bigger.
So many heaped-up dead,
and time gnawing the dead.
And in the ruined houses,
cold disdain and damp.
But he didn't say anything.

The street he used to cross
on horseback, at a gallop.
His watch. His clothes.
His legal documents.
His tales of love-affairs.
Opening of tin trunks
and violent memories.
But he didn't say anything.

In the desert of Itabira
things come back to life,
stiflingly, suddenly.
The market of desires
displays its sad treasures;
my urge to run away;
naked women; remorse.
But he didn't say anything.

Stepping on books and letters
we travel in the family.
Marriages; mortgages;
the consumptive cousins;
the mad aunt; my grandmother
betrayed among the slave-girls,
rustling silks in the bedroom.
But he didn't say anything.

What cruel, obscure instinct
moved his pallid hand
subtly pushing us
into the forbidden
time, forbidden places?

I looked in his white eyes.
I cried to him: Speak! My voice
shook in the air a moment,
beat on the stones. The shadow
proceeded slowly on
with that pathetic travelling
across the lost kingdom.
But he didn't say anything.

I saw grief, misunderstanding
and more than one old revolt
dividing us in the dark.
The hand I wouldn't kiss,
the crumb that they denied me,
refusal to ask pardon.
Pride. Terror at night.
But he didn't say anything.

Speak   speak   speak   speak.
I pulled him by his coat
that was turning into clay.
By the hands, by the boots
I caught at his strict shadow
and the shadow released itself
with neither haste nor anger.
But he remained silent.

There were distinct silences
deep within his silence.
There was my deaf grandfather
hearing the painted birds
on the ceiling of the church;
my own lack of friends;
and your lack of kisses;
there were our difficult lives
and a great separation
in the little space of the room.

The narrow space of life
crowds me up against you,
and in this ghostly embrace
it's as if I were being burned
completely, with poignant love.
Only now do we know each other!
Eye-glasses, memories, portraits
flow in the river of blood.
Now the waters won't let me
make out your distant face,
distant by seventy years . . .

I felt that he pardoned me
but he didn't say anything.
The waters cover his moustache,
the family, Itabira, all.

The Table

(*Carlos Drummond de Andrade*)

And you never liked parties . . .
Old man, what a party
we'd give for you today.
The sons that don't drink
and the one that loves to drink,
around the wide table,
gave up their grim diets,
forgot their likes and dislikes;
it was an honest orgy
ending in revelations.
Yes, old man, you'd hear things
to shock your ninety years.
But then we didn't shock you,
because—what with the smiles,
and the fat hen, and the wine,
good wine from Portugal,
as well as what was made
from a thousand ingredients
and served up in abundance
in a thousand china dishes
—we'd implied already
that it was all in fun.
Yes. Your tired eyes
used to reading the country
in distances of leagues,
and in the distance one steer
lost in the blue blue,
looked into our very souls
and saw their rotten mud,
and sadly stared right through us
and fiercely swore at us
and sweetly pardoned us
(pardon is the usual ritual
for parents, as for lovers).
And then, forgiving all,
you inwardly congratulated

yourself upon such children . . .
Well, the biggest scoundrels
have turned out a lot better
than I bargained for. Besides,
chips off the old . . . You stopped,
frowning suddenly,
inwardly going over
some regretted memory,
and not all that remote,
smiling to yourself, seeing
that you had thrown a bridge
from the grandfather's crazy dance
to the grandsons' escapades,
knowing that all flesh
aspires to degradation,
but on a fiery road
beneath a sexual rainbow,
you coughed. *Harrumph.* Children,
don't be silly. Children?
Great boys in our fifties,
bald, who've been around,
but keeping in our breasts
that young boy's innocence,
that running off to the woods,
that forbidden craving,
and the very simple desire
to ask our mother to mend
more than just our shirts,
our impotent, ragged souls . . .
Ah, it would be a big
*mineiro** dinner . . . We ate,
and hunger grows with eating,
and food was just a pretext.
We didn't even need
to have appetites; everything
was disposed of; the morning after,
we'd take the consequences.
Never disdain *tutu.*†
There goes some more crackling.

*Referring to the State of Minas Gerais.
†Dish made of beans mixed with manioc flour.

As for the turkey? *Farofa**
needs a nice little *cachaça*†
to keep it company,
and don't overlook the beer,
a great companion, too.
The other day . . . Does eating
hold such significance
that the bottom of the dish
alone reveals the best,
most human, of our beings?
Is drinking then so sacred
that only drunk my brother
can explain his resentment
and offer me his hand?
To eat, to drink: what food
more fragrant, more mysterious
than this Portuguese-Arabian,
and what drink is more holy
than this that joins together
such a gluttonous brotherhood,
big-mouths, good fellows all!
And the sister's there who went
before the others, and was
a rose by name, and born
on a day just like today
in order to grace your birthday.
Her name tastes of camelia
and being a rose-amelia,
a much more delicate flower
than any of the rose-roses,
she lived longer than the name,
although she hid, in secret,
the scattered rose. Beside you,
see: it has bloomed again.
The oldest sat down here.
A quiet, crafty type
who wouldn't make a priest,
but liked low love-affairs:
and time has made of him

*Dish made of manioc flour mixed with butter, sausage, eggs, etc.
†Fiery liquor made from sugar cane.

145

what it makes of anyone;
and, without being you,
strangely, the older he grows,
the more he looks like you,
so that if I glimpse him
unexpectedly now
it is you who reappear
in another man of sixty.
This one has a degree,
the diploma of the family,
but his more learned letters
are the writings in the blood
and on the bark of trees.
He knows the names of wildflowers
and remembers those of the rarest
fruits of cross-breeding.
Nostalgia lives in him,
a countryfied city-man,
a scholarly country-man.
He's become a patriarch.
And then you see one who
inherited your hard will
and your hard stoicism.
But he didn't want to repeat you.
He thought it not worth the trouble
to reproduce on the earth
what the earth will swallow up.
He loved. He loves. And will love.
But he doesn't want his love
to be a prison for two,
a contract, between yawns,
and four feet in bedroom slippers.
Passionate at first meeting,
dry, the second time,
agreeable, the third,
one might say he's afraid
of being fatally human.
One might say that he rages,
but that sweetness transcends his rage,
and that his clever, difficult
recourses for fooling himself
about himself exert

a force without a name
unless, perhaps, it's kindness.
One kept quiet, not wanting
to carry on the colloquy,
rustling, subterranean,
of the more talkative ones
with new words of her own.
She kept quiet, you weren't bothered.
If you loved her so much like that,
there's something in her that still
loves you, in the cross-grained way
that suits us. (Not being happy
can explain everything.)
I know, I know how painful
these family occasions are
and to argue at this minute
would be to kill the party
and you—one doesn't die
once, and not forever.
Due to the disagreements
of our blood in the bodies
it runs divided in,
there are always many lives
left to be consumed.
There are always many dead
left to be reincarnated
at length in another dead.
But we are all alive.
And more than alive, joyful.
We are all as we were
before we were, and no one
can say that he didn't get
something from you. For example:
there at the corner of the table,
but not to be humble, perhaps
out of pure vanity
and to show off his awkwardness
in carefully awkward poses,
there you see me. What of it?
Keep calm. Keep calm. I'm working.
After all, the good life
still is only: life

(and neither was it so good,
nor is it so very bad).
Well, that's me. Observe:
I have all the defects
I didn't smoke out in you,
nor do I have those you had,
any more than your qualities.
Never mind: I'm your son
just by being a negative
way of affirming you.
Oh, how we fought and fought!
Wow! It wasn't funny,
but—the paths of love,
only love can track them down.
I gave you such scant pleasure,
none, perhaps . . . unless
I may have given you
a sort of hope of pleasure,
the indifferent satisfaction
of one who feels his son,
just because of being useless,
may turn out to be, at least,
not a bad character.
I'm not a bad character.
If you suspect it, stop;
I'm not any of those things.
Some affections still
can get at my bored heart.
I bore myself? Too much.
That's my trouble. One failing
I didn't inherit from you.
Well, don't keep looking at me,
there are many still to see.
Eight. And all lower-case,
all frustrated. What sadder
flora could we have found
to ornament the table!
But no! Of such remote,
such pure, forgotten ones
on the sucking, transforming earth,
are the angels. How luminous!
Their rays of love shine out,

and among the empty glasses
their glasses clink until
even the shadows reverberate.
They are angels that deign
to participate in the banquet,
to sit on the little stool,
to live a child's life.
They are angels that deign
that a mortal return to God
something of his divine
ethereal, sensitive substance,
if he has, and loses, a child.
Count: fourteen at the table.
Or thirty? Or were there fifty?
How do I know—if more
arrive, daily, one flesh
multiplied and crossed
with other loving flesh?
There are fifty sinners,
if to be born's a sin,
and demonstrate, in sins,
those we were bequeathed.
The procession of your grandsons,
lengthening into great-grandsons,
comes to ask your blessing
and to eat your dinner.
Take notice, for an instant,
of the chin, the look, the gesture,
of the profound conscience,
and of the girlish grace,
and say, if, after all,
there isn't, among my errors,
an unexpected truth.
This is my explanation,
my best or unique verse,
my all, filling my nothing.
And now the table, replete,
is bigger than the house.
We talk with our mouths full,
we call each other names,
we laugh, we split our sides,
we forget the terrible

inhibiting respect,
and all our happiness
blighted in so many black
commemorative banquets
(no use remembering now),
gestures of family affection
accumulated, held back
(no use remembering now),
the kind and gentle words
that said at the right time
could have changed our lives
(no use changing now),
are at table, spreading out
unprecedented food.
Oh, what more celestial supper
and what greater joy on earth!
Who prepared it? What incomparable
vocation for sacrifice
set the table, had the children?
Who was sacrificed? Who paid
the price of all this labor?
Whose was the invisible hand
that traced this arabesque
in flowers around the pudding,
as an aureole is traced?
Who has an aureole? Who
doesn't have one, since
aureoles are gold, and she
wanted to share it quickly,
and with the thought, she did.
Who sits at the left side,
bent over that way? What white,
but what white more than white
target of white hair
draws the color from the oranges,
cancels the coffee, and
outshines the seraphim?
Who is all light and is white?
You had no presentiment
surely, how white can be
a more diverse tinge
of whiteness itself . . . Purity

elaborated in
your absence, and made perfect,
cold, concrete and lunar.
How could our party be
for one and not for two?
Now you are reunited
in a wedding ring much greater
than the simple ring of earth,
together at this table
of wood more lawful* than any
law of the republic.
Now you are above us,
and above this dinner
to which we summoned you
so far—at last—to love you
and loving, delude ourselves
at a table that is

        empty.

*The phrase for hardwood is *madeira de lei*, lawful wood.

From The Death and Life of a Severino
A Pernambuco Christmas Play, 1954–55

(*João Cabral de Melo Neto*)

I

The "Retirante" Explains
to the Reader Who He Is
and What He Does

—My name is Severino,
  I have no Christian name.
  There are lots of Severinos
  (a saint of pilgrimages)
  so they began to call me
  Maria's Severino.
  There are lots of Severinos
  with mothers called Maria,
  so I became Maria's
  of Zacarias, deceased.
  But still this doesn't tell much:
  there are many in the parish
  because of a certain colonel*
  whose name was Zacarias
  who was the very earliest
  senhor of this region.
  Then how explain who's speaking
  to Your Excellencies?
  Let's see: the Severino
  of Maria of Zacarias,
  from the Mountain of the Rib,
  at the end of Paraiba.
  But still this doesn't mean much.
  There were at least five more
  with the name of Severino,
  sons of so many Marias,
  wives of so many other
  Zacariases, deceased,
  living on the same thin,

*"Colonel" means any big land-owner, not necessarily a real colonel.

bony mountain where I lived.
There are lots of Severinos;
we are exactly alike:
exactly the same big head
that's hard to balance properly,
the same swollen belly
on the same skinny legs,
alike because the blood
we use has little color.
And if we Severinos
are all the same in life,
we die the same death,
the same Severino death.
The death of those who die
of old age before thirty,
of an ambuscade before twenty,
of hunger a little daily.
(The Severino death
from sickness and from hunger
attacks at any age,
even the unborn child.)
We are many Severinos
and our destiny's the same:
to soften up these stones
by sweating over them,
to try to bring to life
a dead and deader land,
to try to wrest a farm
out of burnt-over land.
But, so that Your Excellencies
can recognize me better
and be able to follow better
the story of my life,
I'll be the Severino
you'll now see emigrate.

II

He Meets Two Men Carrying a
Corpse in a Hammock and Crying
"Brothers of Souls! Brothers of Souls!
I Didn't Kill Him, Not I!"*

—Whom are you carrying,
    brothers of souls,
  wrapped in that hammock?
    kindly inform me.
—A defunct nobody,
    brother of souls,
  travelling long hours to
    his resting place.
—Do you know who he was,
    brothers of souls?
  Do you know what his name is,
    or what it was?
—Severino Farmer,
    brother of souls,
  Severino Farmer,
    farming no more.
—From where do you bring him,
    brothers of souls?
  Where did you start out
    on your long journey?
—From the driest of lands,
    brother of souls,
  from the land where not even
    wild plants will grow.
—Did he die of this death,
    brothers of souls,
  was it this death he died of,
    or was he killed?

*The "brothers of souls" refrain refers to a religious sect in the north of Brazil—one of whose duties is the burial of pauper dead.

—It wasn't that death,
    brother of souls,
  it was death by killing,
    in ambuscade.
—And who hid in ambush,
    brothers of souls?
  And with what did they kill him,
    a knife or a bullet?
—This was a bullet death,
    brother of souls.
  A bullet's more certain
    (it goes in deeper).
—And who was it ambushed him,
    brothers of souls,
  who let this bullet bird
    out, to harm him?
—That's hard to answer,
    brother of souls,
  there's always a bullet
    idle and flying.
—But what had he done
    brothers of souls,
  what had he done,
    to harm such a bird?
—He owned a few acres,
    brother of souls,
  of stone and leeched sand
    he cultivated.
—But did he have fields,
    brothers of souls,
  how could he plant
    on the barren rock?
—In the thin lips of sand,
    brother of souls,
  in the stones' intervals,
    he planted straw.
—And was his farm big,
    brothers of souls,
  was his farm so big
    that they coveted it?
—He had only two acres,
    brother of souls,

on the mountain's shoulder,
   and neither one level.
—Then why did they kill him,
   brothers of souls,
why did they kill him
   with a shotgun?
—It wanted to spread itself,
   brother of souls,
this bullet bird wanted
   to fly more freely.
—And now what will happen,
   brothers of souls,
will measures be taken
   against that gun?
—It has more space to fly in,
   brother of souls,
more space and more bullets
   to teach to fly.
—And where will you bury him,
   brothers of souls,
with the seed still in him,
   the seed of lead?
—In the graveyard of Torres,
   brother of souls,
(now Toritama)
   at break of day.
—And can I help you,
   brothers of souls,
since I pass Toritama,
   it's on my way.
—Yes, you can help us,
   brother of souls,
it's a brother of souls
   who hears our call.
And then go back,
   brother of souls,
you can go back
   from there to your home.
—I'll go back; it's far,
   brothers of souls,
it's a long day's march
   and the mountain is high.

The defunct is luckier,
   brothers of souls,
since he won't be going
   the long way back.
—Toritama is near,
   brother of souls,
we'll reach holy ground
   by break of day.
—Let's go while it's night,
   brothers of souls,
for the dead's best shroud
   is a starless night.

XIV

(A CHILD HAS JUST BEEN BORN)
Neighbors, Friends, Two Gypsies, et al.
Arrive and Stand Talking in the
Doorway of the Man's House

—All the heaven and earth
    are singing in his praise.
    It was for him the tide
    didn't go out tonight.
—It was for him the tide
    made its motor stop.
    The mud stayed covered up
    and the stench didn't rise.
—And Sargasso lavender,
    acid and disinfectant,
    came to sweep our streets,
    sent from the distant sea.
—And the sponge-dry tongue
    of wind from the interior
    came to suck the moisture
    out of the stagnant puddle.
—All the heaven and earth
    are singing in his praise.
    And every house becomes
    an inviting refuge.
—Every hut becomes
    the kind of ideal refuge
    highly thought of by
    the sociologists.
—The orchestra of mosquitoes
    that broadcasts every night,
    because of him, I think,
    is off the air tonight.

—And this river, always blind,
  opaque from eating dirt,
  that never reflects the sky,
  has adorned itself with stars.

New and Uncollected Work (1969)

Rainy Season; Sub-Tropics

Giant Toad

I am too big, too big by far. Pity me.

My eyes bulge and hurt. They are my one great beauty, even so. They see too much, above, below, and yet there is not much to see. The rain has stopped. The mist is gathering on my skin in drops. The drops run down my back, run from the corners of my downturned mouth, run down my sides and drip beneath my belly. Perhaps the droplets on my mottled hide are pretty, like dewdrops, silver on a moldering leaf? They chill me through and through. I feel my colors changing now, my pigments gradually shudder and shift over.

Now I shall get beneath that overhanging ledge. Slowly. Hop. Two or three times more, silently. That was too far. I'm standing up. The lichen's gray, and rough to my front feet. Get down. Turn facing out, it's safer. Don't breathe until the snail gets by. But we go travelling the same weathers.

Swallow the air and mouthfuls of cold mist. Give voice, just once. O how it echoed from the rock! What a profound, angelic bell I rang!

I live, I breathe, by swallowing. Once, some naughty children picked me up, me and two brothers. They set us down again somewhere and in our mouths they put lit cigarettes. We could not help but smoke them, to the end. I thought it was the death of me, but when I was entirely filled with smoke, when my slack mouth was burning, and all my tripes were hot and dry, they let us go. But I was sick for days.

I have big shoulders, like a boxer. They are not muscle, however, and their color is dark. They are my sacs of poison, the almost unused poison that I bear, my burden and my great responsibility. Big wings of poison, folded on my back. Beware, I am an angel in disguise; my wings are evil, but not deadly. If I will it, the poison could break through, blue-black, and dangerous to all. Blue-black fumes would rise upon the air. Beware, you frivolous crab.

Strayed Crab

This is not my home. How did I get so far from water? It must be over that way somewhere.

I am the color of wine, of *tinta*. The inside of my powerful right claw is saffron-yellow. See, I see it now; I wave it like a flag. I am dapper and elegant; I move with great precision, cleverly managing all my smaller yellow claws. I believe in the oblique, the indirect approach, and I keep my feelings to myself.

But on this strange, smooth surface I am making too much noise. I wasn't meant for this. If I maneuver a bit and keep a sharp lookout, I shall find my pool again. Watch out for my right claw, all passersby! This place is too hard. The rain has stopped, and it is damp, but still not wet enough to please me.

My eyes are good, though small; my shell is tough and tight. In my own pool are many small gray fish. I see right through them. Only their large eyes are opaque, and twitch at me. They are hard to catch, but I, I catch them quickly in my arms and eat them up.

What is that big soft monster, like a yellow cloud, stifling and warm? What is it doing? It pats my back. Out, claw. There, I have frightened it away. It's sitting down, pretending nothing's happened. I'll skirt it. It's still pretending not to see me. Out of my way, O monster. I own a pool, all the little fish that swim in it, and all the skittering waterbugs that smell like rotten apples.

Cheer up, O grievous snail. I tap your shell, encouragingly, not that you will ever know about it.

And I want nothing to do with you, either, sulking toad. Imagine, at least four times my size and yet so vulnerable . . . I could open your belly with my claw. You glare and bulge, a watchdog near my pool; you make a loud and hollow noise. I do not care for such stupidity. I admire compression, lightness, and agility, all rare in this loose world.

Giant Snail

The rain has stopped. The waterfall will roar like that all night. I have come out to take a walk and feed. My body—foot, that is—is wet and cold and covered with sharp gravel. It is white, the size of a dinner plate. I have set myself a goal, a certain rock, but it may well be dawn before I get there. Although I move ghostlike and my floating edges barely graze the ground, I am heavy, heavy, heavy. My white muscles are already tired. I give the impression of mysterious ease, but it is only with the greatest effort of my will that I can rise above the smallest stones and sticks. And I must not let myself be distracted by those rough spears of grass. Don't touch them. Draw back. Withdrawal is always best.

The rain has stopped. The waterfall makes such a noise! (And what if I fall over it?) The mountains of black rock give off such clouds of steam! Shiny streamers are hanging down their sides. When this occurs, we have a saying that the Snail Gods have come down in haste. *I* could never descend such steep escarpments, much less dream of climbing them.

That toad was too big, too, like me. His eyes beseeched my love. Our proportions horrify our neighbors.

Rest a minute; relax. Flattened to the ground, my body is like a pallid, decomposing leaf. What's that tapping on my shell? Nothing. Let's go on.

My sides move in rhythmic waves, just off the ground, from front to back, the wake of a ship, wax-white water, or a slowly melting floe. I am cold, cold, cold as ice. My blind, white bull's head was a Cretan scarehead; degenerate, my four horns that can't attack. The sides of my mouth are now my hands. They press the earth and suck it hard. Ah, but I know my shell is beautiful, and high, and glazed, and shining. I know it well, although I have not seen it. Its curled white lip is of the finest enamel. Inside, it is as smooth as silk, and I, I fill it to perfection.

My wide wake shines, now it is growing dark. I leave a lovely opalescent ribbon: I know this.

But O! I am too big. I feel it. Pity me.

If and when I reach the rock, I shall go into a certain crack there for the night. The waterfall below will vibrate through my shell and body all night long. In that steady pulsing I can rest. All night I shall be like a sleeping ear.

The Hanging of the Mouse

Early, early in the morning, even before five o'clock, the mouse was brought out, but already there were large crowds. Some of the animals had not gone to bed the night before, but had stayed up later and later; at first because of a vague feeling of celebration, and then, after deciding several times that they might as well wander about the town for an hour more, to conclude the night by arriving at the square in time for the hanging became only sensible. These animals hiccupped a little and had an air of cynical lassitude. Those who had got up out of bed to come also appeared weary and silent, but not so bored.

The mouse was led in by two enormous brown beetles in the traditional picturesque armor of an earlier day. They came on to the square through the small black door and marched between the lines of soldiers standing at attention: straight ahead, to the right, around two sides of the hollow square, to the left, and out into the middle where the gallows stood. Before each turn the beetle on the right glanced quickly at the beetle on the left; their traditional long, long antennae swerved sharply in the direction they were to turn and they did it to perfection. The mouse, of course, who had had no military training and who, at the moment, was crying so hard he could scarcely see where he was going, rather spoiled the precision and snap of the beetles. At each corner he fell slightly forward, and when he was jerked in the right direction his feet became tangled together. The beetles, however, without even looking at him, each time lifted him quickly into the air for a second until his feet were untangled.

At that hour in the morning the mouse's gray clothes were almost indistinguishable from the light. But his whimpering could be heard, and the end of his nose was rose-red from crying so much. The crowd of small animals tipped back their heads and sniffed with pleasure.

A raccoon, wearing the traditional black mask, was the executioner. He was very fastidious and did everything just so. One of his young sons, also wearing a black mask, waited on him with a small basin and a pitcher of water. First he washed his hands and rinsed them carefully; then he washed the rope and rinsed it. At the last minute he again washed his hands and drew on a pair of elegant black kid gloves.

A large praying mantis was in charge of the religious end of the ceremonies. He hurried up on the stage after the mouse and his escorts, but once there a fit of nerves seemed to seize him. He glided to the left a few steps, to the right a few steps, lifted his arms gracefully, but could not seem to begin; and it was quite apparent that he would have liked nothing better than to have jumped quickly down and left the whole affair. When his arms were stretched to Heaven his large eyes flashed toward the crowd, and when he looked up, his body was twitching and he moved about in a really pathetic way. He seemed to feel ill at ease with the low characters around him: the beetles, the hangmen, and the criminal mouse. At last he made a great effort to pull himself together and, approaching the mouse, said a few words in a high, incomprehensible voice. The mouse jumped from nervousness, and cried harder than ever.

At this point the spectators would all undoubtedly have burst out laughing, but just then the King's messenger appeared on the balcony above the small black door the mouse and his guards had lately come through. He was a very large, overweight bull-frog, also dressed in the traditional costume and carrying the traditional long scroll that dragged for several feet on the ground and had the real speech, on a little slip of paper, pasted inside it. The scroll and the white plume on his hat made him look comically like something in a nursery tale, but his voice was impressive enough to awe the crowd into polite attention. It was a deep bass: "Glug! Glug! Berrr-up!" No one could understand a word of the mouse's death sentence.

With the help of some pushes and pinches from the beetles, the executioner got the mouse into position. The rope was tied exquisitely behind one of his little round ears. The mouse raised a hand and wiped his nose with it, and most of the crowd interpreted this gesture as a farewell wave and spoke of it for weeks afterwards. The hangman's young son, at a signal from his father, sprang the trap.

"Squee-eek! Squee-eek!" went the mouse.

His whiskers rowed hopelessly round and round in the air a few times and his feet flew up and curled into little balls like young fernplants.

The praying mantis, with an hysterical fling of his long limbs, had disappeared in the crowd. It was all so touching that a cat, who had brought her child in her mouth, shed several large tears. They rolled down on to the child's back and he began to squirm and shriek, so that the mother thought that the sight of the hanging had perhaps been too much for him, but an excellent moral lesson, nevertheless.

1937

Some Dreams They Forgot

The dead birds fell, but no one had seen them fly,
or could guess from where. They were black, their eyes were shut,
and no one knew what kind of birds they were. But
all held them and looked up through the new far-funneled sky.
Also, dark drops fell. Night-collected on the eaves,
or congregated on the ceilings over their beds,
they hung, mysterious drop-shapes, all night over their heads,
now rolling off their careless fingers quick as dew off leaves.
Where had they seen wood-berries perfect black as these,
shining just so in early morning? Dark-hearted decoys on
upper-bough or below-leaf. Had they thought *poison*
and left? or—remember—eaten them from the loaded trees?
What flowers shrink to seeds like these, like columbine?
But their dreams are all inscrutable by eight or nine.

1933

Song

Summer is over upon the sea.
The pleasure yacht, the social being,
that danced on the endless polished floor,
stepped and side-stepped like Fred Astaire,
is gone, is gone, docked somewhere ashore.

The friends have left, the sea is bare
that was strewn with floating, fresh green weeds.
Only the rusty-sided freighters
go past the moon's marketless craters
and the stars are the only ships of pleasure.

1937

House Guest

The sad seamstress
who stays with us this month
is small and thin and bitter.
No one can cheer her up.
Give her a dress, a drink,
roast chicken, or fried fish—
it's all the same to her.

She sits and watches TV.
No, she watches zigzags.
"Can you adjust the TV?"
"No," she says. No hope.
She watches on and on,
without hope, without air.

Her own clothes give us pause,
but she's not a poor orphan.
She has a father, a mother,
and all that, and she's earning
quite well, and we're stuffing
her with fattening foods.

We invite her to use the binoculars.
We say, "Come see the jets!"
We say, "Come see the baby!"
Or the knife grinder who cleverly
plays the National Anthem
on his wheel so shrilly.
Nothing helps.

She speaks: "I need a little
money to buy buttons."
She seems to think it's useless
to ask. Heavens, buy buttons,
if they'll do any good,

the biggest in the world—
by the dozen, by the gross!
Buy yourself an ice cream,
a comic book, a car!

Her face is closed as a nut,
closed as a careful snail
or a thousand-year-old seed.
Does she dream of marriage?
Of getting rich? Her sewing
is decidedly mediocre.

Please! Take our money! Smile!
What on earth have we done?
What has everyone done
and when did it all begin?
Then one day she confides
that she wanted to be a nun
and her family opposed her.

Perhaps we should let her go,
or deliver her straight off
to the nearest convent—and wasn't
her month up last week, anyway?

Can it be that we nourish
one of the Fates in our bosoms?
Clotho, sewing our lives
with a bony little foot
on a borrowed sewing machine,
and our fates will be like hers,
and our hems crooked forever?

Trouvée

for Mr. Wheaton Galentine & Mr. Harold Leeds

Oh, why should a *hen*
have been run over
on West 4th Street
in the middle of summer?

She was a white hen
—red-and-white now, of course.
How did she get there?
Where was she going?

Her wing feathers spread
flat, flat in the tar,
all dirtied, and thin
as tissue paper.

A pigeon, yes,
or an English sparrow,
might meet such a fate,
but not that poor fowl.

Just now I went back
to look again.
I hadn't dreamed it:
there is a hen

turned into a quaint
old country saying
scribbled in chalk
(except for the beak).

Going to the Bakery

[Rio de Janeiro]

Instead of gazing at the sea
the way she does on other nights,
the moon looks down the Avenida
Copacabana at the sights,

new to her but ordinary.
She leans on the slack trolley wires.
Below, the tracks slither between
lines of head-to-tail parked cars.

(The tin hides have the iridescence
of dying, flaccid toy balloons.)
The tracks end in a puddle of mercury;
the wires, at the moon's

magnetic instances, take off
to snarl in distant nebulae.
The bakery lights are dim. Beneath
our rationed electricity,

the round cakes look about to faint—
each turns up a glazed white eye.
The gooey tarts are red and sore.
Buy, buy, what shall I buy?

Now flour is adulterated
with cornmeal, the loaves of bread
lie like yellow-fever victims
laid out in a crowded ward.

The baker, sickly too, suggests
the "milk rolls," since they still are warm
and made with milk, he says. They feel
like a baby on the arm.

Under the false-almond tree's
leathery leaves, a childish *puta*
dances, feverish as an atom:
chá-cha, chá-cha, chá-cha. . . .

In front of my apartment house
a black man sits in a black shade,
lifting his shirt to show a bandage
on his black, invisible side.

Fumes of *cachaça* knock me over,
like gas fumes from an auto-crash.
He speaks in perfect gibberish.
The bandage glares up, white and fresh.

I give him seven cents in *my*
terrific money, say "Good night"
from force of habit. Oh, mean habit!
Not one word more apt or bright?

Under the Window: Ouro Prêto

for Lilli Correia de Araújo

The conversations are simple: about food,
or, "When my mother combs my hair it hurts."
"Women." *"Women!"* Women in red dresses

and plastic sandals, carrying their almost
invisible babies—muffled to the eyes
in all the heat—unwrap them, lower them,

and give them drinks of water lovingly
from dirty hands, here where there used to be
a fountain, here where all the world still stops.

The water used to run out of the mouths
of three green soapstone faces. (One face laughed
and one face cried; the middle one just looked.

Patched up with plaster, they're in the museum.)
It runs now from a single iron pipe,
a strong and ropy stream. "Cold." "Cold as ice,"

all have agreed for several centuries.
Donkeys agree, and dogs, and the neat little
bottle-green swallows dare to dip and taste.

Here comes that old man with the stick and sack,
meandering again. He stops and fumbles.
He finally gets out his enamelled mug.

Here comes some laundry tied up in a sheet,
all on its own, three feet above the ground.
Oh, no—a small black boy is underneath.

Six donkeys come behind their "godmother"
—the one who wears a fringe of orange wool
with wooly balls above her eyes, and bells.

They veer toward the water as a matter
of course, until the drover's mare trots up,
her whiplash-blinded eye on the off side.

A big new truck, Mercedes-Benz, arrives
to overawe them all. The body's painted
with throbbing rosebuds and the bumper says

HERE AM I FOR WHOM YOU HAVE BEEN WAITING.
The driver and assistant driver wash
their faces, necks, and chests. They wash their feet,

their shoes, and put them back together again.
Meanwhile, another, older truck grinds up
in a blue cloud of burning oil. It has

a syphilitic nose. Nevertheless,
its gallant driver tells the passersby
NOT MUCH MONEY BUT IT IS AMUSING.

"She's been in labor now two days." "Transistors
cost much too much." "For lunch we took advantage
of the poor duck the dog decapitated."

The seven ages of man are talkative
and soiled and thirsty.
                    Oil has seeped into
the margins of the ditch of standing water

and flashes or looks upward brokenly,
like bits of mirror—no, more blue than that:
like tatters of the *Morpho* butterfly.

GEOGRAPHY III
(1976)

FOR ALICE METHFESSEL

[From "First Lessons in Geography,"
Monteith's Geographical Series,
A. S. Barnes & Co., 1884]

LESSON VI

What is Geography?
A description of the earth's surface.
What is the Earth?
The planet or body on which we live.
What is the shape of the Earth?
Round, like a ball.
Of what is the Earth's surface composed?
Land and water.

LESSON X

What is a Map?
A picture of the whole, or a part, of the Earth's surface.
What are the directions on a Map?
Toward the top, North; toward the bottom, South; to the right, East;
    to the left, West.
In what direction from the center of the picture is the Island?
North.

In what direction is the Volcano? The Cape? The Bay? The Lake? The Strait?
The Mountains? The Isthmus? What is in the East? In the West? In the South?
In the North? In the Northwest? In the Southeast? In the Northeast? In the
Southwest?

In the Waiting Room

In Worcester, Massachusetts,
I went with Aunt Consuelo
to keep her dentist's appointment
and sat and waited for her
in the dentist's waiting room.
It was winter. It got dark
early. The waiting room
was full of grown-up people,
arctics and overcoats,
lamps and magazines.
My aunt was inside
what seemed like a long time
and while I waited I read
the *National Geographic*
(I could read) and carefully
studied the photographs:
the inside of a volcano,
black, and full of ashes;
then it was spilling over
in rivulets of fire.
Osa and Martin Johnson
dressed in riding breeches,
laced boots, and pith helmets.
A dead man slung on a pole
—"Long Pig," the caption said.
Babies with pointed heads
wound round and round with string;
black, naked women with necks
wound round and round with wire
like the necks of light bulbs.
Their breasts were horrifying.
I read it right straight through.
I was too shy to stop.
And then I looked at the cover:
the yellow margins, the date.

Suddenly, from inside,
came an *oh!* of pain
—Aunt Consuelo's voice—
not very loud or long.
I wasn't at all surprised;
even then I knew she was
a foolish, timid woman.
I might have been embarrassed,
but wasn't. What took me
completely by surprise
was that it was *me:*
my voice, in my mouth.
Without thinking at all
I was my foolish aunt,
I—we—were falling, falling,
our eyes glued to the cover
of the *National Geographic,*
February, 1918.

I said to myself: three days
and you'll be seven years old.
I was saying it to stop
the sensation of falling off
the round, turning world
into cold, blue-black space.
But I felt: you are an *I,*
you are an *Elizabeth,*
you are one of *them.*
Why should you be one, too?
I scarcely dared to look
to see what it was I was.
I gave a sidelong glance
—I couldn't look any higher—
at shadowy gray knees,
trousers and skirts and boots
and different pairs of hands
lying under the lamps.
I knew that nothing stranger
had ever happened, that nothing
stranger could ever happen.

Why should I be my aunt,
or me, or anyone?
What similarities—
boots, hands, the family voice
I felt in my throat, or even
the *National Geographic*
and those awful hanging breasts—
held us all together
or made us all just one?
How—I didn't know any
word for it—how "unlikely" . . .
How had I come to be here,
like them, and overhear
a cry of pain that could have
got loud and worse but hadn't?

The waiting room was bright
and too hot. It was sliding
beneath a big black wave,
another, and another.

Then I was back in it.
The War was on. Outside,
in Worcester, Massachusetts,
were night and slush and cold,
and it was still the fifth
of February, 1918.

Crusoe in England

A new volcano has erupted,
the papers say, and last week I was reading
where some ship saw an island being born:
at first a breath of steam, ten miles away;
and then a black fleck—basalt, probably—
rose in the mate's binoculars
and caught on the horizon like a fly.
They named it. But my poor old island's still
un-rediscovered, un-renamable.
None of the books has ever got it right.

Well, I had fifty-two
miserable, small volcanoes I could climb
with a few slithery strides—
volcanoes dead as ash heaps.
I used to sit on the edge of the highest one
and count the others standing up,
naked and leaden, with their heads blown off.
I'd think that if they were the size
I thought volcanoes should be, then I had
become a giant;
and if I had become a giant,
I couldn't bear to think what size
the goats and turtles were,
or the gulls, or the over-lapping rollers
—a glittering hexagon of rollers
closing and closing in, but never quite,
glittering and glittering, though the sky
was mostly overcast.

My island seemed to be
a sort of cloud-dump. All the hemisphere's
left-over clouds arrived and hung
above the craters—their parched throats
were hot to touch.
Was that why it rained so much?

And why sometimes the whole place hissed?
The turtles lumbered by, high-domed,
hissing like teakettles.
(And I'd have given years, or taken a few,
for any sort of kettle, of course.)
The folds of lava, running out to sea,
would hiss. I'd turn. And then they'd prove
to be more turtles.
The beaches were all lava, variegated,
black, red, and white, and gray;
the marbled colors made a fine display.
And I had waterspouts. Oh,
half a dozen at a time, far out,
they'd come and go, advancing and retreating,
their heads in cloud, their feet in moving patches
of scuffed-up white.
Glass chimneys, flexible, attenuated,
sacerdotal beings of glass . . . I watched
the water spiral up in them like smoke.
Beautiful, yes, but not much company.

I often gave way to self-pity.
"Do I deserve this? I suppose I must.
I wouldn't be here otherwise. Was there
a moment when I actually chose this?
I don't remember, but there could have been."
What's wrong about self-pity, anyway?
With my legs dangling down familiarly
over a crater's edge, I told myself
"Pity should begin at home." So the more
pity I felt, the more I felt at home.

The sun set in the sea; the same odd sun
rose from the sea,
and there was one of it and one of me.
The island had one kind of everything:
one tree snail, a bright violet-blue
with a thin shell, crept over everything,
over the one variety of tree,
a sooty, scrub affair.
Snail shells lay under these in drifts

and, at a distance,
you'd swear that they were beds of irises.
There was one kind of berry, a dark red.
I tried it, one by one, and hours apart.
Sub-acid, and not bad, no ill effects;
and so I made home-brew. I'd drink
the awful, fizzy, stinging stuff
that went straight to my head
and play my home-made flute
(I think it had the weirdest scale on earth)
and, dizzy, whoop and dance among the goats.
Home-made, home-made! But aren't we all?
I felt a deep affection for
the smallest of my island industries.
No, not exactly, since the smallest was
a miserable philosophy.

Because I didn't know enough.
Why didn't I know enough of something?
Greek drama or astronomy? The books
I'd read were full of blanks;
the poems—well, I tried
reciting to my iris-beds,
"They flash upon that inward eye,
which is the bliss . . ." The bliss of what?
One of the first things that I did
when I got back was look it up.

The island smelled of goat and guano.
The goats were white, so were the gulls,
and both too tame, or else they thought
I was a goat, too, or a gull.
Baa, baa, baa and *shriek, shriek, shriek,*
baa . . . shriek . . . baa . . . I still can't shake
them from my ears; they're hurting now.
The questioning shrieks, the equivocal replies
over a ground of hissing rain
and hissing, ambulating turtles
got on my nerves.

When all the gulls flew up at once, they sounded
like a big tree in a strong wind, its leaves.
I'd shut my eyes and think about a tree,
an oak, say, with real shade, somewhere.
I'd heard of cattle getting island-sick.
I thought the goats were.
One billy-goat would stand on the volcano
I'd christened *Mont d'Espoir* or *Mount Despair*
(I'd time enough to play with names),
and bleat and bleat, and sniff the air.
I'd grab his beard and look at him.
His pupils, horizontal, narrowed up
and expressed nothing, or a little malice.
I got so tired of the very colors!
One day I dyed a baby goat bright red
with my red berries, just to see
something a little different.
And then his mother wouldn't recognize him.

Dreams were the worst. Of course I dreamed of food
and love, but they were pleasant rather
than otherwise. But then I'd dream of things
like slitting a baby's throat, mistaking it
for a baby goat. I'd have
nightmares of other islands
stretching away from mine, infinities
of islands, islands spawning islands,
like frogs' eggs turning into polliwogs
of islands, knowing that I had to live
on each and every one, eventually,
for ages, registering their flora,
their fauna, their geography.

Just when I thought I couldn't stand it
another minute longer, Friday came.
(Accounts of that have everything all wrong.)
Friday was nice.
Friday was nice, and we were friends.
If only he had been a woman!
I wanted to propagate my kind,
and so did he, I think, poor boy.

He'd pet the baby goats sometimes,
and race with them, or carry one around.
—Pretty to watch; he had a pretty body.

And then one day they came and took us off.

Now I live here, another island,
that doesn't seem like one, but who decides?
My blood was full of them; my brain
bred islands. But that archipelago
has petered out. I'm old.
I'm bored, too, drinking my real tea,
surrounded by uninteresting lumber.
The knife there on the shelf—
it reeked of meaning, like a crucifix.
It lived. How many years did I
beg it, implore it, not to break?
I knew each nick and scratch by heart,
the bluish blade, the broken tip,
the lines of wood-grain on the handle . . .
Now it won't look at me at all.
The living soul has dribbled away.
My eyes rest on it and pass on.

The local museum's asked me to
leave everything to them:
the flute, the knife, the shrivelled shoes,
my shedding goatskin trousers
(moths have got in the fur),
the parasol that took me such a time
remembering the way the ribs should go.
It still will work but, folded up,
looks like a plucked and skinny fowl.
How can anyone want such things?
—And Friday, my dear Friday, died of measles
seventeen years ago come March.

Night City

[From the plane]

No foot could endure it,
shoes are too thin.
Broken glass, broken bottles,
heaps of them burn.

Over those fires
no one could walk:
those flaring acids
and variegated bloods.

The city burns tears.
A gathered lake
of aquamarine
begins to smoke.

The city burns guilt.
—For guilt-disposal
the central heat
must be this intense.

Diaphanous lymph,
bright turgid blood,
spatter outward
in clots of gold

to where run, molten,
in the dark environs
green and luminous
silicate rivers.

A pool of bitumen
one tycoon
wept by himself,
a blackened moon.

Another cried
a skyscraper up.
Look! Incandescent,
its wires drip.

The conflagration
fights for air
in a dread vacuum.
The sky is dead.

(Still, there are creatures,
careful ones, overhead.
They set down their feet, they walk
green, red; green, red.)

The Moose

for Grace Bulmer Bowers

From narrow provinces
of fish and bread and tea,
home of the long tides
where the bay leaves the sea
twice a day and takes
the herrings long rides,

where if the river
enters or retreats
in a wall of brown foam
depends on if it meets
the bay coming in,
the bay not at home;

where, silted red,
sometimes the sun sets
facing a red sea,
and others, veins the flats'
lavender, rich mud
in burning rivulets;

on red, gravelly roads,
down rows of sugar maples,
past clapboard farmhouses
and neat, clapboard churches,
bleached, ridged as clamshells,
past twin silver birches,

through late afternoon
a bus journeys west,
the windshield flashing pink,
pink glancing off of metal,
brushing the dented flank
of blue, beat-up enamel;

down hollows, up rises,
and waits, patient, while
a lone traveller gives
kisses and embraces
to seven relatives
and a collie supervises.

Goodbye to the elms,
to the farm, to the dog.
The bus starts. The light
grows richer; the fog,
shifting, salty, thin,
comes closing in.

Its cold, round crystals
form and slide and settle
in the white hens' feathers,
in gray glazed cabbages,
on the cabbage roses
and lupins like apostles;

the sweet peas cling
to their wet white string
on the whitewashed fences;
bumblebees creep
inside the foxgloves,
and evening commences.

One stop at Bass River.
Then the Economies—
Lower, Middle, Upper;
Five Islands, Five Houses,
where a woman shakes a tablecloth
out after supper.

A pale flickering. Gone.
The Tantramar marshes
and the smell of salt hay.
An iron bridge trembles
and a loose plank rattles
but doesn't give way.

On the left, a red light
swims through the dark:
a ship's port lantern.
Two rubber boots show,
illuminated, solemn.
A dog gives one bark.

A woman climbs in
with two market bags,
brisk, freckled, elderly.
"A grand night. Yes, sir,
all the way to Boston."
She regards us amicably.

Moonlight as we enter
the New Brunswick woods,
hairy, scratchy, splintery;
moonlight and mist
caught in them like lamb's wool
on bushes in a pasture.

The passengers lie back.
Snores. Some long sighs.
A dreamy divagation
begins in the night,
a gentle, auditory,
slow hallucination. . . .

In the creakings and noises,
an old conversation
—not concerning us,
but recognizable, somewhere,
back in the bus:
Grandparents' voices

uninterruptedly
talking, in Eternity:
names being mentioned,
things cleared up finally;
what he said, what she said,
who got pensioned;

deaths, deaths and sicknesses;
the year he remarried;
the year (something) happened.
She died in childbirth.
That was the son lost
when the schooner foundered.

He took to drink. Yes.
She went to the bad.
When Amos began to pray
even in the store and
finally the family had
to put him away.

"Yes . . ." that peculiar
affirmative. "Yes . . ."
A sharp, indrawn breath,
half groan, half acceptance,
that means "Life's like that.
We know *it* (also death)."

Talking the way they talked
in the old featherbed,
peacefully, on and on,
dim lamplight in the hall,
down in the kitchen, the dog
tucked in her shawl.

Now, it's all right now
even to fall asleep
just as on all those nights.
—Suddenly the bus driver
stops with a jolt,
turns off his lights.

A moose has come out of
the impenetrable wood
and stands there, looms, rather,
in the middle of the road.
It approaches; it sniffs at
the bus's hot hood.

Towering, antlerless,
high as a church,
homely as a house
(or, safe as houses).
A man's voice assures us
"Perfectly harmless. . . ."

Some of the passengers
exclaim in whispers,
childishly, softly,
"Sure are big creatures."
"It's awful plain."
"Look! It's a she!"

Taking her time,
she looks the bus over,
grand, otherworldly.
Why, why do we feel
(we all feel) this sweet
sensation of joy?

"Curious creatures,"
says our quiet driver,
rolling his *r*'s.
"Look at that, would you."
Then he shifts gears.
For a moment longer,

by craning backward,
the moose can be seen
on the moonlit macadam;
then there's a dim
smell of moose, an acrid
smell of gasoline.

12 O'Clock News

gooseneck lamp

As you all know, tonight is the night of the full moon, half the world over. But here the moon seems to hang motionless in the sky. It gives very little light; it could be dead. Visibility is poor. Nevertheless, we shall try to give you some idea of the lay of the land and the present situation.

typewriter

The escarpment that rises abruptly from the central plain is in heavy shadow, but the elaborate terracing of its southern glacis gleams faintly in the dim light, like fish scales. What endless labor those small, peculiarly shaped terraces represent! And yet, on them the welfare of this tiny principality depends.

pile of mss.

A slight landslide occurred in the northwest about an hour ago. The exposed soil appears to be of poor quality: almost white, calcareous, and shaly. There are believed to have been no casualties.

typed sheet

Almost due north, our aerial reconnaissance reports the discovery of a large rectangular "field," hitherto unknown to us, obviously man-made. It is dark-speckled. An airstrip? A cemetery?

envelopes

In this small, backward country, one of the most backward left in the world today, communications are crude and "industrialization" and its products almost nonexistent. Strange to say, however, signboards are on a truly gigantic scale.

We have also received reports of a mysterious, oddly shaped, black structure, at an undisclosed distance to the east. Its presence was revealed only because its highly polished surface catches such feeble moonlight as prevails. The natural resources of the country being far from completely known to us, there is the possibility that this may be, or may contain, some powerful and terrifying "secret weapon." On the other hand, given what we *do* know, or have learned from our anthropologists and sociologists about this people, it may well be nothing more than a *numen*, or a great altar recently erected to one of their gods, to which, in their present historical state of superstition and helplessness, they attribute magical powers, and may even regard as a "savior," one last hope of rescue from their grave difficulties.

ink-bottle

At last! One of the elusive natives has been spotted! He appears to be—rather, to have been—a unicyclist-courier, who may have met his end by falling from the height of the escarpment because of the deceptive illumination. Alive, he would have been small, but undoubtedly proud and erect, with the thick, bristling black hair typical of the indigenes.

typewriter eraser

From our superior vantage point, we can clearly see into a sort of dugout, possibly a shell crater, a "nest" of soldiers. They lie heaped together, wearing the camouflage "battle dress" intended for "winter warfare." They are in hideously contorted positions, all dead. We can make out at least eight bodies. These uniforms were designed to be used in guerrilla warfare on the country's one snow-covered mountain peak. The fact that these poor soldiers are wearing them *here*, on the plain, gives further proof, if proof were necessary, either of the childishness and hopeless impracticality of this inscrutable people, our opponents, or of the sad corruption of their leaders.

ashtray

Poem

About the size of an old-style dollar bill,
American or Canadian,
mostly the same whites, gray greens, and steel grays
—this little painting (a sketch for a larger one?)
has never earned any money in its life.
Useless and free, it has spent seventy years
as a minor family relic
handed along collaterally to owners
who looked at it sometimes, or didn't bother to.

It must be Nova Scotia; only there
does one see gabled wooden houses
painted that awful shade of brown.
The other houses, the bits that show, are white.
Elm trees, low hills, a thin church steeple
—that gray-blue wisp—or is it? In the foreground
a water meadow with some tiny cows,
two brushstrokes each, but confidently cows;
two minuscule white geese in the blue water,
back-to-back, feeding, and a slanting stick.
Up closer, a wild iris, white and yellow,
fresh-squiggled from the tube.
The air is fresh and cold; cold early spring
clear as gray glass; a half inch of blue sky
below the steel-gray storm clouds.
(They were the artist's specialty.)
A specklike bird is flying to the left.
Or is it a flyspeck looking like a bird?

Heavens, I recognize the place, I know it!
It's behind—I can almost remember the farmer's name.
His barn backed on that meadow. There it is,
titanium white, one dab. The hint of steeple,
filaments of brush-hairs, barely there,
must be the Presbyterian church.
Would that be Miss Gillespie's house?

Those particular geese and cows
are naturally before my time.

A sketch done in an hour, "in one breath,"
once taken from a trunk and handed over.
*Would you like this? I'll probably never
have room to hang these things again.
Your Uncle George, no, mine, my Uncle George,
he'd be your great-uncle, left them all with Mother
when he went back to England.
You know, he was quite famous, an R.A. . . .*

I never knew him. We both knew this place,
apparently, this literal small backwater,
looked at it long enough to memorize it,
our years apart. How strange. And it's still loved,
or its memory is (it must have changed a lot).
Our visions coincided—"visions" is
too serious a word—our looks, two looks:
art "copying from life" and life itself,
life and the memory of it so compressed
they've turned into each other. Which is which?
Life and the memory of it cramped,
dim, on a piece of Bristol board,
dim, but how live, how touching in detail
—the little that we get for free,
the little of our earthly trust. Not much.
About the size of our abidance
along with theirs: the munching cows,
the iris, crisp and shivering, the water
still standing from spring freshets,
the yet-to-be-dismantled elms, the geese.

One Art

The art of losing isn't hard to master;
so many things seem filled with the intent
to be lost that their loss is no disaster.

Lose something every day. Accept the fluster
of lost door keys, the hour badly spent.
The art of losing isn't hard to master.

Then practice losing farther, losing faster:
places, and names, and where it was you meant
to travel. None of these will bring disaster.

I lost my mother's watch. And look! my last, or
next-to-last, of three loved houses went.
The art of losing isn't hard to master.

I lost two cities, lovely ones. And, vaster,
some realms I owned, two rivers, a continent.
I miss them, but it wasn't a disaster.

—Even losing you (the joking voice, a gesture
I love) I shan't have lied. It's evident
the art of losing's not too hard to master
though it may look like (*Write* it!) like disaster.

The End of March

for John Malcolm Brinnin and Bill Read: Duxbury

It was cold and windy, scarcely the day
to take a walk on that long beach.
Everything was withdrawn as far as possible,
indrawn: the tide far out, the ocean shrunken,
seabirds in ones or twos.
The rackety, icy, offshore wind
numbed our faces on one side;
disrupted the formation
of a lone flight of Canada geese;
and blew back the low, inaudible rollers
in upright, steely mist.

The sky was darker than the water
—*it* was the color of mutton-fat jade.
Along the wet sand, in rubber boots, we followed
a track of big dog-prints (so big
they were more like lion-prints). Then we came on
lengths and lengths, endless, of wet white string,
looping up to the tide-line, down to the water,
over and over. Finally, they did end:
a thick white snarl, man-size, awash,
rising on every wave, a sodden ghost,
falling back, sodden, giving up the ghost. . . .
A kite string?—But no kite.

I wanted to get as far as my proto-dream-house,
my crypto-dream-house, that crooked box
set up on pilings, shingled green,
a sort of artichoke of a house, but greener
(boiled with bicarbonate of soda?),
protected from spring tides by a palisade
of—are they railroad ties?
(Many things about this place are dubious.)
I'd like to retire there and do *nothing*,
or nothing much, forever, in two bare rooms:
look through binoculars, read boring books,

old, long, long books, and write down useless notes,
talk to myself, and, foggy days,
watch the droplets slipping, heavy with light.
At night, a *grog à l'américaine.*
I'd blaze it with a kitchen match
and lovely diaphanous blue flame
would waver, doubled in the window.
There must be a stove; there *is* a chimney,
askew but braced with wires,
and electricity, possibly
—at least, at the back another wire
limply leashes the whole affair
to something off behind the dunes.
A light to read by—perfect! But—impossible.
And that day the wind was much too cold
even to get that far,
and of course the house was boarded up.

On the way back our faces froze on the other side.
The sun came out for just a minute.
For just a minute, set in their bezels of sand,
the drab, damp, scattered stones
were multi-colored,
and all those high enough threw out long shadows,
individual shadows, then pulled them in again.
They could have been teasing the lion sun,
except that now he was behind them
—a sun who'd walked the beach the last low tide,
making those big, majestic paw-prints,
who perhaps had batted a kite out of the sky to play with.

Objects & Apparitions

for Joseph Cornell

Hexahedrons of wood and glass,
scarcely bigger than a shoebox,
with room in them for night and all its lights.

Monuments to every moment,
refuse of every moment, used:
cages for infinity.

Marbles, buttons, thimbles, dice,
pins, stamps, and glass beads:
tales of the time.

Memory weaves, unweaves the echoes:
in the four corners of the box
shadowless ladies play at hide-and-seek.

Fire buried in the mirror,
water sleeping in the agate:
solos of Jenny Colonne and Jenny Lind.

"One has to commit a painting," said Degas,
"the way one commits a crime." But you constructed
boxes where things hurry away from their names.

Slot machine of visions,
condensation flask for conversations,
hotel of crickets and constellations.

Minimal, incoherent fragments:
the opposite of History, creator of ruins,
out of your ruins you have made creations.

Theatre of the spirits:
objects putting the laws
of identity through hoops.

"Grand Hotel de la Couronne": in a vial,
the three of clubs and, very surprised,
Thumbelina in gardens of reflection.

A comb is a harp strummed by the glance
of a little girl
born dumb.

The reflector of the inner eye
scatters the spectacle:
God all alone above an extinct world.

The apparitions are manifest,
their bodies weigh less than light,
lasting as long as this phrase lasts.

Joseph Cornell: inside your boxes
my words became visible for a moment.

Translated from the Spanish of Octavio Paz.

Five Flights Up

Still dark.
The unknown bird sits on his usual branch.
The little dog next door barks in his sleep
inquiringly, just once.
Perhaps in his sleep, too, the bird inquires
once or twice, quavering.
Questions—if that is what they are—
answered directly, simply,
by day itself.

Enormous morning, ponderous, meticulous;
gray light streaking each bare branch,
each single twig, along one side,
making another tree, of glassy veins . . .
The bird still sits there. Now he seems to yawn.

The little black dog runs in his yard.
His owner's voice arises, stern,
"You ought to be ashamed!"
What has he done?
He bounces cheerfully up and down;
he rushes in circles in the fallen leaves.

Obviously, he has no sense of shame.
He and the bird know everything is answered,
all taken care of,
no need to ask again.
—Yesterday brought to today so lightly!
(A yesterday I find almost impossible to lift.)

NEW AND
UNCOLLECTED POEMS
(1978–1979)

Santarém

Of course I may be remembering it all wrong
after, after—how many years?

That golden evening I really wanted to go no farther;
more than anything else I wanted to stay awhile
in that conflux of two great rivers, Tapajós, Amazon,
grandly, silently flowing, flowing east.
Suddenly there'd been houses, people, and lots of mongrel
riverboats skittering back and forth
under a sky of gorgeous, under-lit clouds,
with everything gilded, burnished along one side,
and everything bright, cheerful, casual—or so it looked.
I liked the place; I liked the idea of the place.
Two rivers. Hadn't two rivers sprung
from the Garden of Eden? No, that was four
and they'd diverged. Here only two
and coming together. Even if one were tempted
to literary interpretations
such as: life/death, right/wrong, male/female
—such notions would have resolved, dissolved, straight off
in that watery, dazzling dialectic.

In front of the church, the Cathedral, rather,
there was a modest promenade and a belvedere
about to fall into the river,
stubby palms, flamboyants like pans of embers,
buildings one story high, stucco, blue or yellow,
and one house faced with *azulejos*, buttercup yellow.
The street was deep in dark-gold river sand
damp from the ritual afternoon rain,
and teams of zebus plodded, gentle, proud,
and *blue*, with down-curved horns and hanging ears,
pulling carts with solid wheels.
The zebus' hooves, the people's feet
waded in golden sand,

dampered by golden sand,
so that almost the only sounds
were creaks and *shush, shush, shush.*

Two rivers full of crazy shipping—people
all apparently changing their minds, embarking,
disembarking, rowing clumsy dories.
(After the Civil War some Southern families
came here; here they could still own slaves.
They left occasional blue eyes, English names,
and *oars*. No other place, no one
on all the Amazon's four thousand miles
does anything but paddle.)
A dozen or so young nuns, white-habited,
waved gaily from an old stern-wheeler
getting up steam, already hung with hammocks
—off to their mission, days and days away
up God knows what lost tributary.
Side-wheelers, countless wobbling dugouts . . .
A cow stood up in one, quite calm,
chewing her cud while being ferried,
tipping, wobbling, somewhere, to be married.
A river schooner with raked masts
and violet-colored sails tacked in so close
her bowsprit seemed to touch the church

(Cathedral, rather!). A week or so before
there'd been a thunderstorm and the Cathedral'd
been struck by lightning. One tower had
a widening zigzag crack all the way down.
It was a miracle. The priest's house right next door
had been struck, too, and his brass bed
(the only one in town) galvanized black.
Graças a deus—he'd been in Belém.

In the blue pharmacy the pharmacist
had hung an empty wasps' nest from a shelf:
small, exquisite, clean matte white,
and hard as stucco. I admired it
so much he gave it to me.
Then—my ship's whistle blew. I couldn't stay.

Back on board, a fellow-passenger, Mr. Swan,
Dutch, the retiring head of Philips Electric,
really a very nicc old man,
who wanted to see the Amazon before he died,
asked, "What's that ugly thing?"

1978

North Haven

in memoriam: Robert Lowell

I can make out the rigging of a schooner
a mile off; I can count
the new cones on the spruce. It is so still
the pale bay wears a milky skin, the sky
no clouds, except for one long, carded horse's-tail.

The islands haven't shifted since last summer,
even if I like to pretend they have
—drifting, in a dreamy sort of way,
a little north, a little south or sidewise,
and that they're free within the blue frontiers of bay.

This month, our favorite one is full of flowers:
Buttercups, Red Clover, Purple Vetch,
Hawkweed still burning, Daisies pied, Eyebright,
the Fragrant Bedstraw's incandescent stars,
and more, returned, to paint the meadows with delight.

The Goldfinches are back, or others like them,
and the White-throated Sparrow's five-note song,
pleading and pleading, brings tears to the eyes.
Nature repeats herself, or almost does:
repeat, repeat, repeat; revise, revise, revise.

Years ago, you told me it was here
(in 1932?) you first "discovered *girls*"
and learned to sail, and learned to kiss.
You had "such fun," you said, that classic summer.
("Fun"—it always seemed to leave you at a loss . . .)

You left North Haven, anchored in its rock,
afloat in mystic blue . . . And now—you've left
for good. You can't derange, or re-arrange,
your poems again. (But the Sparrows can their song.)
The words won't change again. Sad friend, you cannot change.

1978

Pink Dog

[Rio de Janeiro]

The sun is blazing and the sky is blue.
Umbrellas clothe the beach in every hue.
Naked, you trot across the avenue.

Oh, never have I seen a dog so bare!
Naked and pink, without a single hair . . .
Startled, the passersby draw back and stare.

Of course they're mortally afraid of rabies.
You are not mad; you have a case of scabies
but look intelligent. Where are your babies?

(A nursing mother, by those hanging teats.)
In what slum have you hidden them, poor bitch,
while you go begging, living by your wits?

Didn't you know? It's been in all the papers,
to solve this problem, how they deal with beggars?
They take and throw them in the tidal rivers.

Yes, idiots, paralytics, parasites
go bobbing in the ebbing sewage, nights
out in the suburbs, where there are no lights.

If they do this to anyone who begs,
drugged, drunk, or sober, with or without legs,
what would they do to sick, four-leggèd dogs?

In the cafés and on the sidewalk corners
the joke is going round that all the beggars
who can afford them now wear life preservers.

In your condition you would not be able
even to float, much less to dog-paddle.
Now look, the practical, the sensible

solution is to wear a *fantasía*.*
Tonight you simply can't afford to be a-
n eyesore. But no one will ever see a

dog in *máscara* this time of year.
Ash Wednesday'll come but Carnival is here.
What sambas can you dance? What will you wear?

They say that Carnival's degenerating
—radios, Americans, or something,
have ruined it completely. They're just talking.

Carnival is always wonderful!
A depilated dog would not look well.
Dress up! Dress up and dance at Carnival!

1979

*Carnival costume.

Sonnet

Caught—the bubble
in the spirit-level,
a creature divided;
and the compass needle
wobbling and wavering,
undecided.
Freed—the broken
thermometer's mercury
running away;
and the rainbow-bird
from the narrow bevel
of the empty mirror,
flying wherever
it feels like, gay!

1979

UNCOLLECTED POEMS
(1933–1969)

The Flood

It finds the park first, and the trees
    turn wavery and wet;
but all the extinguished traffic knows
    that it will drown the steeples yet.

The battered houses, rows of brick,
    are clear as quartz; the color thins
to amethyst,—the chimney-pots
    and weather-vanes stick up like fins.

And slowly down the fluid streets
    the cars and trolleys, goggle-eyed,
enamelled bright like gaping fish,
    drift home on the suburban tide.

Along the airy upper beach
    to the minutely glittering sky
two sand-pipers have stepped, and left
    four star-prints high and dry.

Beyond the town, subaqueous,
    the green hills change to green-mossed shells;
and at the church, to warn the ships above,
    eight times they ring the bells.

1933

A Word with You

Look out! there's that damned ape again
sit silently until he goes,
or else forgets the things he knows
(whatever they are) about us, then
we can begin to talk again.

Have you tried playing with your ring?
Sometimes that calms them down, I find.
(Bright objects hypnotize the mind.)
Get his attention on anything—
anything will do—there, try your ring.

The glitter pleases him. You see
he squints his eyes; his lip hangs loose.
You were saying?—Oh Lord, what's the use,
for now the parrot's after me
and the monkeys are awake. You see

how hard it is, you understand
this nervous strain in which we live—
Why just one luscious adjective
infuriates the whole damned band
and they're squabbling for it. I understand

some people manage better. How?
They treat the creatures without feeling.
—Throw books to stop the monkeys' squealing,
slap the ape and make him bow,
are firm, keep order,—but I don't know how.

Quick! there's the cockatoo! he heard!
(He can't bear any form of wit.)
—Please watch out that you don't get bit;
there's not a thing escapes that bird.
Be silent,—now the ape has overheard.

1933

Hymn to the Virgin

Pull back the curtains, quick now that we've caught the mood of
Adoration's shamefaced exposé and brazen knee-bending.
Let's see, and quick about it, God's-beard, Christ's crown, baby-brood of
Strawberry ice-cream colored cherubim, tin-winged, ascending
Chub-toes a'dangle earthwards, fat-fists a-pat-a-cake for Thee, oh
    wooed of
Erstwhile eye-raised mortals! Show where you've been spending
Storage years in that great attic, all the red plush portieres food of
Sacramenting moths, and all the gilded ropes and tassels spotted
By the doers-of-the-Word flies, midst magnificence and plunder rotted!

    Pull back, pull back
    And through the crack
Glimpse of the dusty grandeur, faith's fall'n paraphernalia rise!
Ah, on the dais of the dazzled, dust-beclouded skies
    Come, Blessed Mary, stand on air,
    Rorate coeli desuper,
Strike on our senses strong again with smell-stale incense, *Ave* cries
And reds and blues and golden-oaks. We aeroplane-wise raise our eyes!

    We know a thing or two
        Mary, Mary,
    Which we will tell to You,
        Mary, Mary.

    As you once housed the Truth
        Belly-within,
    Whom else should we tell it to,
        You, without-sin?

    In its due season
        From Thy pure portals
    Sans rhyme or reason
        Truth came. We mortals

Intrust now wistfully
         Into Thy tender side
Our Truth, to keep, till it
         Gets itself crucified.

Glor'ous effulgence—
         Time cannot dim it,
Alpha and Omega,
         Thou art the Limit.

Ah! wouldst not, wax-faced, wooden-bodied one, have us to
    worship us-wise?
Turn not aside Thy pretty-painted face, parade and meet our
    audience-eyes you must.
Long-hardened candle-grease about Thy feet, and tarnished
    dimes and nickels, thus-wise
Did previous paltry penny-clinkers come, but we bear ark-like
    our great trust.
What, take it not? Oh petulant and cranky princess, shall we
    force it on Thee lust-wise?
We cannot bear to draw the curtains back, leave Thee to
    barrenness and rouging rust.

         Come, Blessed Mary, hear our prayer!
         Come, Blessed Mary, stand on air—
         Rorate coeli desuper!

1933

Three Sonnets for the Eyes

I / *Tidal Basin*

Withdrawing water would be thus discreet
So as to make us think 'twas in our mind
—That sickening rupture happening there. "How blind
Are eyes!" says it, (dragging its slippery feet)
"Now they're left vacant truths, like angel eyes on
The old gravestones; seeing into the graves.
Your own heart beat your own eyes' color to waves
And filléd blue this full to the horizon."

Oh wait! off there it mends revenge on colors, gains
Brilliantest interest on its interrupted wealth . . .
Soon it all the awful socket'll flesh to health,
Over the sunk sides steal its iris sweet blue veins.
Sight from the senses not thus easy's sprung. And see
Thine eyes new-spheréd, held whole, shine to thee!

II

They all kept looking at each other's eyes,
Look, here I am, in here! you're warm—oh look again!
I knew you knew all else there gaped in vain:
Stared eyes dull, wide-winked, squinted wrong surmise
And ours said nothing, nothing; dumb mediator
To them that glance and turned cheek from its sweep
And single smile: (second of unbroken nightlong sleep
Misunderstood by day) its instant own translator.

The birds cried all, descending on the elms
As if t'uproot them, carry them by storm and singing.
The wind dropped stiff; an armored sun went ringing
Down ground, 's gold splintered. Evening overwhelms,
We thought (I knew *we*) 't fortunately covers
With lashes, lids of reticence, these eyes those lovers.

III

Thy senses are too different to please me—
Touch I might touch; whole the split difference
On twenty fingers' tips. But hearing's thence
Long leagues of thee, where wildernesses increase . . . See
Flesh-forests, nerve-vined, pain-star-blossom full,
Trackless to where trembles th'ears' eremite.
And where from there a stranger turns to sight?
Thine eyes nest, say, soft shining birds in the skull?

Either above thee or thy gravestone's graven angel
Eyes I'll stand and stare. The secret's in the forehead
(Rather the structure's gap) once you are dead.
They leave that way together, no more strange. I'll
Look in lost upon those neatest nests of bone
Where steel-coiled springs have lashed out, fly-wheels flown.

1933

Three Valentines

I

Love with his gilded bow and crystal arrows
    Has slain us all,
Has pierced the English sparrows
Who languish for each other in the dust,
While from their bosoms, puffed with hopeless lust,
    The red drops fall.

The robins' wings fan fev'rish arcs and swirls
    Attempting hugs,
While Venus pats her darling's curls
And just to polish off his aim, suggests
Some unrequited passions in the breasts
    Of am'rous bugs.

See, up there, pink and plump and smug in sashes,
    The little bastard grin,
Watching the pretty rainbows on his lashes . . .
Oh sweet, sweet Love—go kick thy naughty self
Around a cloud, or prick thy naughty self
    Upon a gilded pin.

II

Now a conundrum Love propounds
    My heart:
You with himself my Love confounds
    With perfect art,
Until I swear I cannot tell you two apart.

One year ago too well I knew
    Dissimilarity
Between my foolish Love and you.
    —What charity
From you, or Love, made up my Love's disparity?

Into your image now my Love has grown,
    Your size,
And even every feature like. I own
    Surprise
To meet, when I meet you—or Love—your eyes.

Nor does an eyelash differ; nor a hair
    But's shaped exactly
To you I love, and warns me to beware
    My dubious security,
—Sure of my love, and Love; uncertain of identity.

But poor Love's imitation's made him mute
    In his perfection.
Announced to you, upon your most minute
    Inspection
You'd think but that you met your own reflection.

Such curious Love, in constant innocence,
    Though ill at ease,
Admits, between you and himself, no difference
    And no degrees . . .
I sometimes pride me on Love's limitations, they being these.

III

Love is feathered like a bird
    To keep him warm,
    To keep him safe from harm,
And by what winds or drafts his nest is stirred
    They chill not Love.
        Warm lives he:
    No warmth gives off,
        Or none to me.

Claws he has like any hawk
    To clutch and keep,
    To clutch so he may sleep
While round the red heart's perch his claws can lock
    And fasten Love.
        His hold he'll not resign,

Nor from the heart fall off,
    Or not from mine.

At nights the grackle Love will start
    To shriek and shrill,
    Nor will he once be still
Till he has wide awake the backward heart.
    So selfish Love,
        Go hush;
    Feathers and claws take off
        Or seek some bush.

1934

The Reprimand

If you taste tears too often, inquisitive tongue,
You'll find they've something you'd not reckoned on;
Crept childish out to touch eye's own phenomenon,
Return, into your element. Tears belong
To only eyes; their deepest sorrow they wrung
From water. Where wept water's gone
That residue is sorrow, salt and wan,
Your bitter enemy, who leaves the face white-strung.

Tears, taster, have a dignity in display,
Carry an antidotal gift for drying.
Unsuited to a savoring by the way,
Salt puckers tear-drops up, ends crying.
Oh curious, cracked and chapped, now will you say,
Tongue, "Grief's not mine" and bend yourself to sighing?

1935

The Mountain

At evening, something behind me.
I start for a second, I blench,
or staggeringly halt and burn.
I do not know my age.

In the morning it is different.
An open book confronts me,
too close to read in comfort.
Tell me how old I am.

And then the valleys stuff
impenetrable mists
like cotton in my ears.
I do not know my age.

I do not mean to complain.
They say it is my fault.
Nobody tells me anything.
Tell me how old I am.

The deepest demarcations
can slowly spread and fade
like any blue tattoo.
I do not know my age.

Shadows fall down, lights climb.
Clambering lights, oh children!
you never stay long enough.
Tell me how old I am.

Stone wings have sifted here
with feather hardening feather.
The claws are lost somewhere.
I do not know my age.

I am growing deaf. The birdcalls
dwindle. The waterfalls
go unwiped. What is my age?
Tell me how old I am.

Let the moon go hang,
the stars go fly their kites.
I want to know my age.
Tell me how old I am.

1952

The Wit

"Wait. Let me think a minute," you said.
And in the minute we saw:
Eve and Newton with an apple apiece,
and Moses with the Law,
Socrates, who scratched his curly head,
and many more from Greece,
all coming hurrying up to now,
bid by your crinkled brow.

But then you made a brilliant pun.
We gave a thunderclap of laughter.
Flustered, your helpers vanished one by one;
and through the conversational spaces, after,
we caught,—back, back, far, far,—
the glinting birthday of a fractious star.

1956

Exchanging Hats

Unfunny uncles who insist
in trying on a lady's hat,
—oh, even if the joke falls flat,
we share your slight transvestite twist

in spite of our embarrassment.
Costume and custom are complex.
The headgear of the other sex
inspires us to experiment.

Anandrous aunts, who, at the beach
with paper plates upon your laps,
keep putting on the yachtsmen's caps
with exhibitionistic screech,

the visors hanging o'er the ear
so that the golden anchors drag,
—the tides of fashion never lag.
Such caps may not be worn next year.

Or you who don the paper plate
itself, and put some grapes upon it,
or sport the Indian's feather bonnet,
—perversities may aggravate

the natural madness of the hatter.
And if the opera hats collapse
and crowns grow draughty, then, perhaps,
he thinks what might a miter matter?

Unfunny uncle, you who wore a
hat too big, or one too many,
tell us, can't you, are there any
stars inside your black fedora?

Aunt exemplary and slim,
with avernal eyes, we wonder
what slow changes they see under
their vast, shady, turned-down brim.

1956

A Norther—Key West

Like little blackbirds in the street
the little Negroes lift their feet,
      the sidewalks freeze;

the tin roofs all look frozen, too,
the flowers blackened, and how blue
      the big palm trees!

While steadily the norther churns
the pale-green sea until it turns
      to lime milk sherbet,

and careful mother Mizpah Oates
brings out the ancient winter coats
      for Hannibal and Herbert,

once worn by an immense white child.
She drives her gentle children wild
      by her obtuseness.

Hannibal weeps. Oh, tragedy!
The waist hangs almost to his knee!
      Oh, worldliness!

1962

Thank-You Note

[in the "Harvard Advocate"]

Mr. Berryman's songs and sonnets say:
"Gather ye berries harsh and crude while yet ye may."
Even if they pucker our mouths like choke-cherries,
Let us be grateful for these thick-bunched berries.

1969

UNCOLLECTED
TRANSLATIONS
(1950–1975)

Rainbow

(Max Jacob)

It was the hour when night makes the mountains lament
And the crags creak under the footsteps of animals,
The birds flew away from the countryside like poison
To get to the sea, to get to a better horizon.
Pursuing a poet then the devil went.
The poet stared at the sea as if he were dead,
For there the sea powdered the edge of a bay
And covered the skin of the giant rocks with scales.
But Jesus, with fire shining behind his head,
Came to climb up the black crags, bearing the cross.
The poet stretched out his arms towards the Savior
And everything vanished: the somber night and the beasts.
The poet followed God for his happiness.

1950

Patience of an Angel

(Max Jacob)

You can beat me, beat me! beat me, said the demon who stood near the stoup of holy water, but you cannot destroy me. I am the rebel angel but I am an angel and my face that you so often mar bears at least the trace of one virtue: patience. You can beat me! beat me! My time will come.

1950

Banks

(Max Jacob)

I complain like the flute,
Always the same tune
No rests in the water-cress
The toad sounding "do"
Would prefer the bassoon.

Elves whose forces beguile
Must I, for my part,
Go to bed all my life
Dreaming of greater Art?

So many stops and looks
But never any listens
For a poor man who traps
A snowstorm that glistens.

1950

Hell Is Graduated

(Max Jacob)

When I was employed at Cooperative Fashions, in spite of the dark, ugly old maid, I tried to steal some garters. I was pursued down the superb staircases, not for the theft, but for my laziness at work and for my hatred of the innocent finery. Descend, you are pursued. The staircases are less beautiful in the offices than in the part open to the public. The staircases are less beautiful in the "service" quarters than in the offices. The staircases are still less beautiful in the cellar! But what can I say of the marsh where I arrived? What can I say of the laughter? Of the animals that brushed by me, and of the whisperings of unseen creatures? Water gave place to fire, to fear, to unconsciousness; when I came to myself I was in the hands of silent and nameless surgeons.

1950

My Last Poem

(Manuel Bandeira)

I would like my last poem thus

That it be gentle saying the simplest and least intended things
That it be ardent like a tearless sob
That it have the beauty of almost scentless flowers
The purity of the flame in which the most limpid diamonds are
    consumed
The passion of suicides who kill themselves without explanation.

1972

Brazilian Tragedy

(*Manuel Bandeira*)

Misael, civil servant in the Ministry of Labor, 63 years old,

Knew Maria Elvira of the Grotto: prostitute, syphilitic, with ulcerated fingers, a pawned wedding ring and teeth in the last stages of decay.

Misael took Maria out of "the life," installed her in a two-storey house in Junction City, paid for the doctor, dentist, manicurist. . . . He gave her everything she wanted.

When Maria Elvira discovered she had a pretty mouth, she immediately took a boy-friend.

Misael didn't want a scandal. He could have beaten her, shot her, or stabbed her. He did none of these: they moved.

They lived like that for three years.

Each time Maria Elvira took a new boy-friend, they moved.

The lovers lived in Junction City. Boulder. On General Pedra Street, The Sties. The Brickyards. Glendale. Pay Dirt. On Marquês de Sapucaí Street in Villa Isabel. Niterói. Euphoria. In Junction City again, on Clapp Street. All Saints. Carousel. Edgewood. The Mines. Soldiers Home . . .

Finally, in Constitution Street, where Misael, bereft of sense and reason, killed her with six shots, and the police found her stretched out, supine, dressed in blue organdy.

1972

Cemetery of Childhood

(Joaquim Cardozo)

[Children's Week, 1953]

In the cemetery of Childhood
It was morning when I entered,
The flowers were in bloom,
So many I was dazzled . . .
It was morning, bright with dew,
When I reached my own country,
Of the smiling faces I saw
I'll remember very few.

From wide distances
My horse travelled swiftly,
Through night, across the night,
Searching by after-glow;
And I heard, ominous,
A remote, forgotten voice . . .
And the roosters crow and crow
—Sunrise sunflowers.

From behind those mountains,
Through the leagues of summer,
How many repeated steps
Tracking the same ground;
And along the roadsides:
Rosary, cross, and heart . . .
Women praying tears,
Their hands telling the drops.

Here the wings of the angels
Fell off. Homely paths
Adorn the small graves
With thorns and white nettles;
My steps came closer, closer,
Too close, stealthily:
The souls flew up from the ground:
A flock of little birds.

Oh! the small afflictions
In the hearts of toys!
Your sleeping rosebushes
Drop their leaves in fright . . .
Your grief brings evening dew,
Sweetness of early morning;
Oh! cemetery of Childhood,
Reveal your secret light.

Flesh, ash, and earth
Feed mortal mysteries;
Children, then adults:
The big fields of cane . . .
Like a king's ransom
Berries load the trees,
Cattle graze the levels
Of the vast common plain.

1971

Elegy for Maria Alves

(Joaqim Cardozo)

I bring you now these flowers
—Modest flowers of an October sun—
Flowers from old hedgerows, flowers from bramble bushes,
Verbenas and everlastings, jasmines and mignonettes;
Colors of the sky in far-off twilights
And the transparency and limpidity of afternoons
When girls dreamed in the gazebos
In ancient gardens at the city's edge.

The fruits that I place on the ground, your ground,
Wrapped in this philodendron leaf
(Daughters, too, of a sun you did not see)
Are wild guavas, plums from native hedges,
Surinam cherries, star-apples, queens' hearts;
They are red, they are fragrant and yellow
As if they were . . . as if still blossoms . . .

The earths that I scatter
Over the earth of your empty body
Come from far away:
Sands from Sweet River and from Piety,
Red grains from the shores of the sea,
Potters' clays from the "Ruins of Palmyra" with their colors
Of rainbow shipwrecked on the hills of Olinda.

Thus, Maria, I bring you flowers, fruits, and earths . . .
And to keep them always fresh and pure,
Over them I pour these waters,
Sweet and clear, mild and friendly:
Water from the Sluice of Apipucos,
Water from the Fount of the Rosary
—Relics of ancient rains—
Waters wept for me, for you, for all of us.

1972

Infancy

(Carlos Drummond de Andrade)

My father got on his horse and went to the field.
My mother stayed sitting and sewing.
My little brother slept.
A small boy alone under the mango trees,
I read the story of Robinson Crusoe,
the long story that never comes to an end.

At noon, white with light, a voice that had learned
lullabies long ago in the slave-quarters—and never forgot—
called us for coffee.
Coffee blacker than the black old woman
delicious coffee
good coffee.

My mother stayed sitting and sewing
watching me:
Shh—don't wake the boy.
She stopped the cradle when a mosquito had lit
and gave a sigh . . . how deep!
Away off there my father went riding
through the farm's endless wastes.

And I didn't know that my story
was prettier than that of Robinson Crusoe.

1972

In the Middle of the Road

(Carlos Drummond de Andrade)

In the middle of the road there was a stone
there was a stone in the middle of the road
there was a stone
in the middle of the road there was a stone.

Never should I forget this event
in the life of my fatigued retinas.
Never should I forget that in the middle of the road
there was a stone
there was a stone in the middle of the road
in the middle of the road there was a stone.

1972

Family Portrait

(Carlos Drummond de Andrade)

Yes, this family portrait
is a little dusty.
The father's face doesn't show
how much money he earned.

The uncles' hands don't reveal
the voyages both of them made.
The grandmother's smoothed and yellowed;
she's forgotten the monarchy.

The children, how they've changed.
Peter's face is tranquil,
that wore the best dreams.
And John's no longer a liar.

The garden's become fantastic.
The flowers are gray badges.
And the sand, beneath dead feet,
is an ocean of fog.

In the semicircle of armchairs
a certain movement is noticed.
The children are changing places,
but noiselessly! it's a picture.

Twenty years is a long time.
It can form any image.
If one face starts to wither,
another presents itself, smiling.

All these seated strangers,
my relations? I don't believe it.
They're guests amusing themselves
in a rarely-opened parlor.

Family features remain
lost in the play of bodies.
But there's enough to suggest
that a body is full of surprises.

The frame of this family portrait
holds its personages in vain.
They're there voluntarily,
they'd know how—if need be—to fly.

They could refine themselves
in the room's chiaroscuro,
live inside the furniture
or the pockets of old waistcoats.

The house has many drawers,
papers, long staircases.
When matter becomes annoyed,
who knows the malice of things?

The portrait does not reply,
it stares; in my dusty eyes
it contemplates itself.
The living and dead relations

multiply in the glass.
I don't distinguish those
that went away from those
that stay. I only perceive
the strange idea of family

travelling through the flesh.

1972

Sonnet of Intimacy

(*Vinícius de Moraes*)

Farm afternoons, there's much too much blue air.
I go out sometimes, follow the pasture track,
Chewing a blade of sticky grass, chest bare,
In threadbare pajamas of three summers back,

To the little rivulets in the river-bed
For a drink of water, cold and musical,
And if I spot in the brush a glow of red,
A raspberry, spit its blood at the corral.

The smell of cow manure is delicious.
The cattle look at me unenviously
And when there comes a sudden stream and hiss

Accompanied by a look not unmalicious,
All of us, animals, unemotionally
Partake together of a pleasant piss.

1971

Four Sambas

(*Anonymous*)

[In Rio de Janeiro, dozens of new sambas are composed for each year's Carnival. Although sambas concerning love outnumber all others, there are always some about world events, such as landing on the moon, and Brazilian politics and life in general. This sampling from 1965, a year after the "rightist" revolution, comments on, or pokes fun at power failures, government turnovers, and the hopelessly bad urban trains.]

Rio de Janeiro,
My joy and my delight!
By day I have no water,
By night I have no light.

Kick him out of office!
He's a greedy boy!
I've nothing to investigate,
What I want is joy!
Justice has arrived.
"Pull" won't work again.
Some have fled to Uruguay;
Some have fled to Spain!

Marshál, Illustrious Marshál,*
Consider the problem
Of the suburbs on the Centrál!
I'm sorry for poor Juvenál,
Hanging in the old Centrál
All year long . . .
He works in Leblon
And lives in Delight†
And gets to work mornings
Late at night.
Oh, Marshál!

Come, my mulata,
    Take me back!
You're the joker
    In my pack,

*The then President, Castelo Branco.
†Opposite ends of the city: the first, rich; the second, working-class.

The prune in my pudding,
    Pepper in my pie,
My package of peanuts,
    The moon in my sky.

1965/1975

The Key of Water

(*Octavio Paz*)

After Rishikesh
the Ganges is still green.
The glass horizon
breaks among the peaks.
We walk upon crystals.
Above and below
great gulfs of calm.
In the blue spaces
white rocks, black clouds.
You said:
>   *Le pays est plein de sources.*
That night I laved my hands in your breasts.

1972

Translated by Elizabeth Bishop with the author.

Along Galeana Street

(*Octavio Paz*)

Hammers pound there above
    pulverized voices
From the top of the afternoon
    the builders come straight down

We're between blue and good evening
    here begin vacant lots
A pale puddle suddenly blazes
    the shade of the hummingbird ignites it

Reaching the first houses
    the summer oxidizes
Someone has closed the door someone
    speaks with his shadow

It darkens   There's no one in the street now
    not even this dog
scared to walk through it alone
    One's afraid to close one's eyes

        Mexico, 18 June 1971

1972

Translated by Elizabeth Bishop with the author.

The Grove

(Octavio Paz)

Enormous and solid
                  but swaying,
beaten by the winds
                  but chained
to the soil,
           murmur of millions of leaves
against the window:
                the inextricable
mass
    woven dark green branches
and dazzling spaces.
               Fallen
into these nets
            there's a material
violent, resplendent,
             an animal
wrathful and swift,
              now immobile,
light that lights itself
               to extinguish itself.
To the left, above the wall,
                more idea than color,
the blue blue of a basin
             edged round by large rocks,
crumbling,
        sand silently precipitated
into the funnel of the grove.
               In the central
part
    thick drops of ink
             spattered
on a sheet of paper inflamed by the west,
                  black
there, almost entirely,
             in the far southeast,

where the horizon breaks down.
                                    The grove
turns copper, shines.
                        Three blackbirds
pass through the blaze and reappear,
                                        unharmed,
in an emptiness: neither light nor shade.
                                    Vegetation
on fire for its dissolution.
                            In the houses
lights are lit.
                    In the window
the sky gathers.
                        In its walls of tile
the patio
            grows more and more
secluded:
            it perfects
its reality.
            And now
on the opaque cement
                        nothing but
sackfuls of shadow
                    the trash-can,
the empty flower-pot.
                        Space closes
over itself:
            inhuman.
Little by little, the names petrify.

Cambridge, England, 28 July 1970

1972

Translated by Elizabeth Bishop with the author.

January First

(Octavio Paz)

The year's doors open
like those of language,
toward the unknown.
Last night you told me:
                     tomorrow
we shall have to think up signs,
sketch a landscape, fabricate a plan
on the double page
of day and paper.
Tomorrow, we shall have to invent,
once more,
the reality of this world.

I opened my eyes late.
For a second of a second
I felt what the Aztec felt,
on the crest of the promontory,
lying in wait
for time's uncertain return
through cracks in the horizon.

But no, the year had returned.
It filled all the room
and my look almost touched it.
Time, with no help from us,
had placed
in exactly the same order as yesterday
houses in the empty street,
snow on the houses,
silence on the snow.

You were beside me,
still asleep.
The day had invented you
but you hadn't yet accepted
being invented by the day.

—Nor possibly my being invented, either.
You were in another day.

You were beside me
and I saw you, like the snow,
asleep among appearances.
Time, with no help from us,
invents houses, streets, trees
and sleeping women.

When you open your eyes
we'll walk, once more,
among the hours and their inventions.
We'll walk among appearances
and bear witness to time and its conjugations.
Perhaps we'll open the day's doors.
And then we shall enter the unknown.

Cambridge, Mass., 1 January 1975

1975

Translated by Elizabeth Bishop with the author.

APPENDIX I: Selected Unpublished
Manuscript Poems

APPENDIX II: Contents of Elizabeth Bishop's
Books of Poetry on First Publication, 1946–1977

Index of Titles and First Lines

APPENDIX I: Selected Unpublished Manuscript Poems

A NOTE ON THE TEXT

Elizabeth Bishop foresaw that some of her uncompleted work might be published after her death. Her will grants her literary executors "power to determine whether any of my unpublished manuscripts and papers shall be published and, if so, to see them through the press." The selection here was made in consultation with Frank Bidart, her surviving literary executor, and Jonathan Galassi, her publisher. The poems are reproduced in facsimile so that the reader can see exactly how finished, or unfinished, Bishop left them. Each facsimile is accompanied by straightforward transcription of the poem the page contains. Titles have been regularized. Instructions as to revisions are followed where these can be confidently interpreted. Canceled words (indicated with a strikethrough) and marginal alternatives (enclosed in square brackets) are retained only where such questions appear unresolved. Additional words, phrases, and lines appearing in the margins on the manuscript page have not been transcribed.

Drafts of unpublished poems by Elizabeth Bishop in this edition are drawn from the Vassar College Libraries Special Collections (hereafter Vassar), the Houghton Library at Harvard University (hereafter Houghton), the Rosenbach Museum and Library (hereafter Rosenbach), and two private collections.

Good-Bye –

You are leaving the earth
but only a little distance
a handbreadth, your flight –
a running has of your hand
lost on the earth, would describe it –
but just that much is so hard to do,
it has cost centuries of effort,
and is costing no centuries of grief.
In the late, crowded, terminal
we both look mostly, idle,
yours golondrin over late shelbies.

Have a martini. The great effort is yet to begin.

On eyes blan & wry
slightly teorfet
in our last on a half-real gaye night –
til let me see, in the end,
in this noisy restaurant –
just of the mots widow
a the heavy wine slow
it want to regrete
it will deposit you like a surd –

hold on

hold on, as I love you –

[1931-34]

Good-Bye —

You are leaving the earth
but only a little distance
a hairsbreadth, your flight —
or a short /curving/ hair of your head
laid on the earth, would describe it —
but just that much is so hard to do,
it has cost other ~~people~~ centuries of effort
and is costing us centuries of grief.
In the hot, crowded, terminal
wc both look smaller, older,
your gabardine suit looks shabbier.
Have a martini. The great effort is yet to begin.
Our eyes bleary & / /
slightly tearful
we made lists on a half-wet paper napkin —
What are we, in this mob,
in this noisy restaurant —
just at the misty window
the /slick/ heavy wings slow
it wants to /migrate/
it will deposit you like a seed —
hold on
hold on, as I lose you —

Dated by Vassar "[1931–34]" (Vassar 64.3); published in *Edgar Allan Poe & The Juke-Box*. Due
to the state of the manuscript, some words are barely legible (and are enclosed in slashes in
the transcription). In line 4, Alice Quinn offers "curly"; in line 11, "you're" has been read as
"your"; no satisfactory interpretation of the word in line 13 has been found; in line 19, Quinn
also offers "slick"; in line 20, Quinn offers "negotiate."

We went to the dark cave of the street-corner
And the kiosk was bare.
A cold wind drove the people off the streets
Then flew their doors ajar.
But two white-faced angel-newsboys
With black mouths were there,
With their sparkled wing-sheaves of newspapers,
And they prophesied "War! War!"

Then we noticed a bright light
At the end of the street where we stood,
And we saw that the street stretched to Africa
Where a round African sun burned red.
There in the hot sands of the Circus
Sad, sand-colored lions stood,
And in the middle of the Circus was
An ancient Roman fountain, filled with blood.

"We went to the dark cave of the street-corner . . ."

We went to the dark cave of the street-corner
And the kiosk was bare.
A cold wind drove the people off the streets
Then blew their doors ajar.
But two white-faced angel-newsboys
With black mouths were there,
With their speckled wing-sheaves of newspapers,
And they prophesied "War! War!"

Then we noticed a bright light
At the end of the street where we stood,
And we saw that the street stretched to Africa
Where a round African sun burned red.
There in the hot sands of the Circus
Sad, sand-colored lions stood,
And in the middle of the Circus was
An ancient Roman fountain, filled with blood.

Dated in Bishop's hand "1935   36?" (Vassar 72A.2, p. 50); published in *Edgar Allan Poe &*
The Juke-Box.

IN A ROOM

~~~~ , 1936

There was an ~~enormous~~ stain on the ceiling
        Over the bed,
        Shaped like a rhinoceros head
With a jagged horn and a trumpet in his mouth.
    //The trumpet had blown, without "feeling,"

    the ~~awful~~ gilt plaster-work, hoarsely,
        From his jaw.
        In the morning I saw   h,s?
Over my head the brilliant results of ~~the~~ music:
    //A molding, constructed as coarsely

        As an opera-house balustrade.
        ~~Then,~~ Off-center because
        ~~that had been~~ one room now was
three or four rooms of unequal sizes,
        the chandelier displayed

        Its large, branched star, snow-flake plan,
        Brassy-gold,
        But with no lamp to hold.
Also Under the molding the two rusted pipes
        the plumbing arrangements ran

        to the closet in the corner and ~~then~~ bored
        Within it.
        Several times every minute
the toilet trickled and splashed, ~~and~~ occasionally (flushed)
        of its own ~~hobgoblin~~ accord.

        The floor was of dark red stones, damp and uneven.
        Near one wall
    — ~~for no reason at all~~
a heavy iron chain hung half-way down from the ceiling,
giving a medieval sensation of heaven.

        One electric light bulb alone was provided.
        Under the light
        Perpetually, day and night,
All the time I ~~lived~~ there, five flies held a dance.
In unhurried orbits they glided

In a Room

There was a stain on the ceiling
    Over the bed,
    Shaped like a rhinoceros head
With a jagged horn and a trumpet in his mouth.
    The trumpet had blown, without "feeling,"

All the gilt plaster-work, hoarse,
    From his jaw.
    In the morning I saw
Over my head the brilliant results of the music: [his?]
    A molding, coarse

As an opera-house balustrade.
    Off-center because
    What was one room now was
Three or four rooms of unequal sizes,
    The big chandelier displayed

Its large, branched star, snow-flake plan,
    Brassy-gold,
    But with no lamp to hold.
Under the molding the two rusted pipes
    Of the plumbing arrangements ran

To the closet in the corner and bored
    Within it.
    Several times every minute
The hobgoblin toilet trickled and splashed,
    Flushed of its own accord.

The floor was dark red stone, damp and uneven.
    Near one wall
    ~~for no reason at all~~
a heavy iron chain hung half-way down from the ceiling,
    giving a medieval sensation of heaven.

Like five planets, only ~~together~~ the both back and forwards:
    On the track
    They let themselves drift ~~buzzing~~ back,
Then began again. Their sound was a boring sentence
Emphasized over and over on the wrong words.

I dried my stockings on the balcony and kept
    Untidy piles
    Of newspapers on the red tiles   shelf ?
In the beautiful white marble fire-place, with its ~~mantle~~
Upheld on scallop shells. At night I slept

On the great lumpy bed, in a range of mountains,
    and had
    — the ~~most remarkably~~ bad   sensibly bad ?
Dreams of my ~~whole~~ life, while from the water-closet
Came ~~the~~ sounds of far-off squalls and fountains.

When not sleeping, I observed that
    All night
    Fine gold whiskers of light
Spread over the ceiling from the next room, pricking out
That molding, like a curious cat.

A man and his wife sat up late in there; I could hear
    them fighting
    In low voices, and a continuous writing,
"Scratch - scratch - scratch," going on, while they drank
Bottle after bottle of beer.

In the darkness ~~the~~ the five flies spoke
    Of Revelations
    In their hopeless conversations,
Of the gilded beauties of heaven, and the blackness of hell, too,
                                 till thinking
    "But here I am in my room," I awoke.

AND MY CAT

lived in the room with me.
                       echo

E. Bishop

the waters speak:

my cat, my cat
where are you looking at?

One electric light bulb alone was provided.
        Under the light
        Perpetually, day and night,
All the time I lived there, five flies held a dance.
        In unhurried orbits they glided

        Like five planets, only they both ~~went~~ back and forwards:
        On their track
        They let themselves drift back,
Then began again. Their sound was a boring sentence
        Emphasized over and over on the wrong words.

        I dried my stockings on the balcony and kept
        Untidy piles
        Of newspapers on the red tiles
In the beautiful white marble fire-place, with its ~~mantle~~   [shelf?]
        Upheld on scallop shells. At night I slept

        On the great lumpy bed, in a range of mountains,
        and had
        ~~the most remarkably~~ bad   [remarkably bad?]
Dreams of my life, while from the water-closet
        Came sounds of far-off squalls and fountains.

        When not sleeping, I observed that
        All night
        Fine gold whiskers of light
Spread over the ceiling from the next room, pricking out
        That molding, like a curious cat.

        A man and his wife stayed up late in there; I could hear
        Them fighting
        In low voices, and a continuous writing,
"Scratch—scratch—scratch," going on, while they drank
        Bottle after bottle of beer.

In the darkness ~~the~~ five flies spoke   [my] [the]
    Of Revelations
  In their hopeless conversations,
Of the gilded beauties of heaven, and the blackness of hell,
                 too, till thinking
  "But here I am in my room," I awoke.

Dated in Bishop's hand "Seville 1936" (Vassar 64.6); published in *Edgar Allan Poe & The Juke-Box.*

Designs like this all over the furniture — supposed to be set with enamels jewels

---

TO BE WRITTEN ON THE MIRROR IN WHITEWASH

I live only here, between your eyes and you,
But I live in your world. What do I do?
—Collect no interest — otherwise what I can;
Above all, I am not that staring man,

To Be Written on the Mirror
in Whitewash

I live only here, between your eyes and you,
But I live in your world, What do I do?
—Collect no interest—otherwise what I can;
Above all, I am not that staring man.

c. 1937 (Vassar 75.46, p.50). Another copy was enclosed in an envelope to Marianne Moore on November 5, 1937, without a covering letter (Rosenbach, V:04:31); published in *The Complete Poems, 1927–1979*.

THE ~~REAR~~ STREET BY THE CEMETERY

The people on little verandahs in the moonlight
are looking at the graveyard
like passengers on ship-board.
How did it happen on this warm & brilliant night
that steerage passengers
were given deck chairs?

They are admiring the long row of white boarders
inside the graveyard paling.
The moon goes sailing,
and hypnotized they sit on the verandahs
with nothing much to say
to the neighbors three feet away.

The gravestones do not move; lit in the fleeting motions
of the shade
its white blossoms etc
like piece of paper in those dark accumulations
floating in a cluster
in the dirty harbor.

for Bone Key

The Street by the Cemetery

The people on little verandahs in the moonlight
    are looking at the graveyard
    like passengers on ship-board.
How did it happen on this warm & brilliant night
    that steerage passengers
    were given deck-chairs?

They are admiring the long row of white oleanders
    inside the graveyard paling.
    The moon goes sailing,
and hypnotized they sit on the verandahs
    with nothing much to say
    to the neighbors three feet away.

The gravestones do not move; but in the blended motions
    of the oleander
    its white blossoms stir
like pieces of paper in those dark accumulations
    floating in a cluster
    in the dirty harbor.

c. 1941 (Vassar 75.4b, p. 227); published in *Edgar Allan Poe & The Juke-Box.*

~~The pale child with the silver hair~~
for A. B.

The pale child with silky hair
Sat on the sofa all afternoon
And in the softest Southern accent
Read Hans Christian Andersons,

And laughed half-scared and too high-pitched
Showing pallid little gums;
Cried because the Snow-Queen come,
Her temples hollowed with bad dreams.

~~Except~~ for the interrupted story:
The woodcarver's child who grew so weary,
The frozen dwarf in white, the orphan
The child who died and lay in the white coffin.

For A.B.

The pale child with silver hair
Sat on the sofa all afternoon
And in the softest Southern accent
Read Hans Christian Andersen,

And laughed half-scared and too high-pitched
Showing pallid little gums;
Cried because the Snow-Queen came,
Her temples hollowed with bad dreams,

Wept for the interrupted story:
The woodsman's child who grew so weary,
The Princess dressed in white, the orphan,
The child who died and lay in the white coffin.

c. 1930s (Vassar 75.4, p. 233); published in *Edgar Allan Poe & The Juke-Box*. "A.B." is Arthur Bulmer.

In the walled-off swimming-pool the water is perfectly flat.
The pink Seurat bathers are dipping themselves in and out
Through a pane of blueish glass.
The cloud reflections pass,
With their amoeba-motions directly through
The beds of bathing caps: white, lavendar, and chalk-blue.
The sky turns gray, the water turns opaque,
Pistachio green and Mermaid Milk.
But out among the keys
Where the water goes its own way, the shallow pleasure seas
Drift this way and that mingling their currents and tides
In all the colors that swarm across the sides
Of soap-bubbles, poisonous and fabulous.
The keys float lightly like rolls of green dust.
From an airplane the water is like a sheet
Of glass over a crumbling bas-relief:
Clay-yellow coral and purple dulces.
And the long, submerged green grass.
it a wide shadow pulses.
The water is a burning-glass
Turned to the sun,
it cools and blues as the afternoon wears on,
And liquidly floats
Floats weeds, surrounds fish, supports a violently red bell-bouy
Whose neon-color vibrates on the water, whose bells vibrate
Over the water glittering rhythmically
As if shocks of electricity passed through it.
It is a sea of delight. The sea means room.
It is a dance-floor, an airy ball-room.
From the swimming-pool or from the deck of a ship
Pleasures strike off and skip
Over the glittering surface; A Grief floats off
Spreading out thin like oil; And Love
Sets out determinedly in a straight line,
One of his burning ideas in mind,
Keeping his eyes on
The bright horizon,
But shatters almost immediately, suffers through refraction,
Comes back in fans, in sheaves of suggestion.
Happy the people in the swimming-pool and on the yacht,
Happy the man in the airplane, likely as not -
And out there where the coral reef comes up in a shelf
The water runs at it, leaps, throws itself
Lightly, lightly, whitening in the air:
An acre of cold white spray is there
Dancing happily by itself.

Pleasure Seas

In the walled-off swimming-pool the water is perfectly flat.
The pink Seurat bathers are dipping themselves in and out
Through a pane of blueish glass.
The cloud reflections pass
Huge amoeba-motions directly through
The beds of bathing caps: white, lavender, and blue.
If the sky turns gray, the water turns opaque,
Pistachio green and Mermaid Milk.
But out among the keys
Where the water goes its own way, the shallow pleasure seas
Drift this way and that mingling currents and tides
In most of the colors that swarm around the sides
Of soap-bubbles, poisonous and fabulous.
& The keys float lightly like rolls of green dust.
From an airplane the water's a heavy sheet
Of glass above a bas-relief:
Clay-yellow coral and purple dulces
And long, leaning, submerged green grass.
Across it a wide shadow pulses.
The water is a burning-glass
Turned to the sun
That blues and cools as the afternoon wears on,
And liquidly
Floats weeds, surrounds fish, supports a violently red bell-buoy
Whose neon-color vibrates over it, whose bells vibrate
Through it. It glitters rhythmically
To shock after shock of electricity.
The sea is delight. The sea means *room*.
It is a dance-floor, a well-ventilated ball-room.
From the swimming-pool or from the deck of a ship
Pleasures strike off humming, skip
Over the ~~glittering~~ surface. A Grief floats off   [tinsel?]
Spreading out thin like oil: And Love
Sets out determinedly in a straight line,
One of his burning ideas in mind,
Keeping his eyes on

The bright horizon,
But shatters immediately, suffers refraction,
And comes back in shoals of distraction.
Happy the people in the swimming-pool and on the yacht,
Happy the man in that airplane, likely as not—
And out there where the coral reef ~~comes up~~ in a shelf
The water runs at it, leaps, throws itself
Lightly, lightly, whitening in the air:
An acre of cold white spray is there
Dancing happily by itself.

c. 1939, only surviving copy of a poem sold to *Harper's Bazaar* in 1940 but never printed (Vassar 60.8); published in *The Complete Poems, 1927–1979*.

It is marvellous to wake up together
At the same minute; marvellous to hear
The rain begin suddenly all over the roof,
To feel the air suddenly clear
As if electricity had passed through it
From a black mesh of wires in the sky.
All over the roof the rain hisses,
And below, the light falling of kisses.

An electrical storm is coming or moving away;
It is the prickling air that wakes us up.
If lightening struck the house now, it would run
From the four blue china balls on top
Down the roof and down the rods all around us,
And we imagine dreamily
How the whole house caught in a bird-cage of lightning
Would be quite delightful rather than frightening;

And from the same simplified point of view
Of night and lying flat on one's back
All things might change equally easily,
Since always to warn us there must be these black
Electrical wires dangling. Without surprise
The world might change to something quite different,
 As the air changes or the lightning comes without our blinking,
Change as our kisses are changing without our thinking.

"It is marvellous to wake up together . . ."

It is marvellous to wake up together
At the same minute; marvellous to hear
The rain begin suddenly all over the roof,
To feel the air suddenly clear
As if electricity had passed through it
From a black mesh of wires in the sky.
All over the roof the rain hisses,
And below, the light falling of kisses.

An electrical storm is coming or moving away;
It is the prickling air that wakes us up.
If lightning struck the house now, it would run
From the four blue china balls on top
Down the roof and down the rods all around us,
And we imagine dreamily
How the whole house caught in a bird-cage of lightning
Would be quite delightful rather than frightening;

And from the same simplified point of view
Of night and lying flat on one's back
All things might change equally easily,
Since always to warn us there must be these black
Electrical wires dangling. Without surprise
The world might change to something quite different,
   As the air changes or the lightning comes without our blinking,
Change as our kisses are changing without our thinking.

c. 1941–46 (Vassar 75.2); published in *Edgar Allan Poe & The Juke-Box*.

EDGAR ALLAN POE & THE JUKE-BOX

The juke-box burns; the music falls
nearly through the darkened room
...bright, La Conga, all the dance-halls
in the block of honkey-tonks,
cavities in our aching moon,
strung with bottles and blue lights
and silvered coconuts and corals.

As easily as the music falls,
the nickels fall into the slots,
the drinks like lonely water-falls
in night descend the separate throats,
and the hands fall on one another,
darker darkness ...
... tolls. ... everything descends,
descends, falls, — much as we envision
the helpless earthward fall of love
descending from the head and eye
down to the hand, and heart, and down.
The music pretends to laugh and weep
while it descends to drink and murder.
The burning box can keep the measure
strict, always, and the ... on down — God.

... said that poetry was ...
But ... phrases on mechanics
... know beforehand what they want
and know exactly what they want.
Do they obtain their single effect?
... can be calculated like alcohol
or like the response to the nickels.
— just how long does the music burn?
like poetry, or all your tunes
half as ... as tunes here?

blue as gas,
blue as the ...
of a blind man's eye

Edgar Allan Poe & The Juke-Box

Easily through the darkened room
the music falls; the juke-box burns.
Starlight, La Conga, all the dance-halls
in the block of honkey-tonks,
cavities in our waning moon,
strung with bottles and blue lights
and silvered coconuts and conches.

As easily as the music falls,
the nickels fall into the slots,
the drinks like lonely water-falls
in night descend the separate throats,
and the hands fall on one another
darker darkness under
tablecloths & all descends,
descends, falls,—much as we envision
the helpless earthward fall of love
descending from the head and eye
down to the hands, and heart, and down.
The music pretends to laugh and weep
while it descends to drink and murder.
The burning box can keep the measure
strict, always, and the down-beat.

Poe said that poetry was *exact.*
But pleasures are mechanical
and know beforehand what they want
and know exactly what they want.
& they obtain that single effect
that can be calculated like alcohol
or like the response to the nickel.
—how long does the music burn?
like poetry, or all your horror
half as exact as horror here?

1940s (Vassar 75.b, p. 239); published in *Edgar Allan Poe & The Juke-Box.*

E. Bishop
623 Margaret St.
Key West, Florida

THE SOLDIER AND THE SLOT-MACHINE

I will not play the slot-machine.
  Don't force the nickle in my hand.
I will not play the slot-machine
  For all the nickles in the land.

I will not ask for change again.
  The barkeeper can see me dead
Before I'll try to meet those eyes
  That move like money in his head.

The slot-machine is all embossed
  With horns of plenty done in gilt;
And out of them all down its front
  Stream dummy coins supposedly spilt,

Like medals for its cleverness,
  As if the slot-machine could cough
In nickles down its tunic, but
  One cannot pick the dummies off.

They are symbolic of the whole
  It seems to me, and I should know
Since hundreds of times, thousands of times,
  I've added mine onto that row

Moving along here in this groove
  Towards that hole they all fall through.
The slot-machine is who is drunk
  And you're a dirty nickle, too...

Its notions all are preconceived.
  It tempts one much to tear apart
The metal frame, to investigate
  The workings of its metal heart,

The grindings of its metal brain,
  The bite of its decisive teeth.
Oh yes, they decorate the top
  But not the awful underneath.

The slot-machine is full of ----.
  The slot-machine's materiel
And if you squint your eyes it looks
  A little like a general.

The Soldier and the Slot-Machine

I will not play the slot-machine.
    Don't force the nickel in my hand.
I will not play the slot-machine
    For all the nickels in the land.

I will not ask for change again.
    The barkeeper can see me dead
Before I'll try to meet those eyes
    That move like money in his head.

The slot-machine is all embossed
    With horns of plenty done in gilt;
And out of them all down its front
    Stream dummy coins supposedly spilt,

Like medals for its cleverness,
    As if the slot-machine could cough
In nickels down its tunic, but
    One cannot pick the dummies off.

They are symbolic of the whole
    It seems to me, and I should know
Since hundreds of times, thousands of times,
    I've added mine onto that row

Moving along here in this groove
    Towards that hole they all fall through.
The slot-machine is who is drunk
    And you're a dirty nickel, too . . .

Its notions all are preconceived.
    It tempts one much to tear apart
The metal frame, to investigate
    The workings of its metal heart,

And even if generously inclined
  Its money all will melt, I'm sure,
And flow like mercury through the cracks
  And make a pool beneath the floor...

It should be flung into the sea.
  It should be broken up for junk
And all its nickles taken away.
  The slot-machine is who is drunk.

I will not play the slot-machine.
  It's pleasures I cannot afford.
Whoever got the Twin Jack-Pot?
  Whoever won the Gold Award?

The grindings of its metal brain,
    The bite of its decisive teeth.
Oh yes, they decorate the top
    But not the awful underneath.

The slot-machine is full of ———.
    The slot-machine's materiel
And if you squint your eyes it looks
    A little like a general.

And even if generously inclined
    Its money all will melt, I'm sure,
And flow like mercury through the cracks
    And make a pool beneath the floor . . .

It should be flung into the sea.
    It should be broken up for junk
And all its nickels taken away.
    The slot-machine is who is drunk.

I will not play the slot-machine.
    Its pleasures I cannot afford.
Whoever got the Twin Jack-Pot?
    Whoever won the Gold Award?

c. 1942 (Vassar 64.7); published in *Edgar Allan Poe & The Juke-Box*. In line 46, "its" has been read for "it's".

I had a bad dream
toward morning, about you.
you lay unconscious
It was to be
for "24 ho.
Wrapped in a long blanket
I felt I must hold you
even though a "bed of guest"
might come in from the garden
at a minute.
I see us lying
with my arms around you
& my cheek on yours.
It was warm — but I had to
pull you
from slipping away
from your body, your cheek
from the wound-round blanket.
                          grows dark morning

Thinking of you
a thousand miles away,
how I tried to hold you
with the mineral arms of a dream

        in the deep of the morning
                        the day coming
that loneliness like filling a
    the sidewalk in a crowd
that fills one in with shade. so
                slow, absolute slow.
the sidewalk rises, rises
like absolute despair

"I had a bad dream . . ."

I had a bad dream,
toward morning, about you.
You lay unconscious
It was to be
for "24 hrs."
Wrapped in a long blanket
I felt I must hold you
even though a "load of guests"
might come in from the garden
/at/ a minute
& see us lying
with my arms around you
& my cheek on yours.
It was warm—but I had to
prevent you
from slipping away
from your body your cheek
from the wound-round blanket—
      grave dark morning
Thinking of you
a thousand miles away,
how I tried to hold you
with the numb arms of a dreamer

  in the deep of the morning
            the day coming
that loneliness like falling on
  the sidewalk in a crowd
that fills some slow, elaborate shame.
the sidewalk rises rises
like absolute despair

n.d. (Vassar 75.3b, p. 167); published in *Edgar Allan Poe & The Juke-Box*. The word at the start of line 10 may be "at," as in the phrase "at a minute's notice."

P. Bishop
Yaddo
Saratoga Springs, N.Y.

THE OWL'S JOURNEY

Somewhere the owl rode on the rabbit's back
down a long slope, over the long, dried grasses,
through a half-moonlight igniting everything
with specks of faintest blue & green, .
They made no sound, no shriek, no Whoo!
- off on a long-forgotten journey.
- The adventure's miniature and ancient:
a collaboration thought up by a child.
But they obliged, and off they went together,
the owl's claws locked deep in the rabbit's fur,
not hurting him, and the owl seated
a little sideways, his mind on something else;
the rabbit's ears laid back, his eyes intent.
But the dream never got any further.

[handwritten marginal notes, largely illegible]

The Owl's Journey

Somewhere the owl rode on the rabbit's back
down a long slope, over the long, dried grasses,
through a half-moonlight igniting everything
with specks of faintest green & blue.
They made no sound, no shriek, no *Whoo!*
—off on a long-forgotten journey.
—The adventure's miniature and ancient:
collaboration thought up by a child.
But they obliged, and off they went together.
The owl's claws lock deep in the rabbit's fur,
and the owl seated
a little sideways, his mind on something else;
the rabbit's ears are back, his eyes intent.
    —But the dream has never got any further.

c. 1949–50 (Vassar, 64.10); published in *Edgar Allan Poe & The Juke-Box*.

Where are the dolls who loved me so
when I was young?
Who cared for me with hands of bisque,
poked breadcrumbs in between my lips,

 Where are the~~se~~ early nurses,
Gertrude, Zilpha, and Nokomis?

Through their real eyes   *six*

                                                        n

 blank ~~crotches~~ crotches,
and ~~fake~~ wri~~st~~t-watches,
whose hands moved only when they wanted -

 Their stocis/m ~~that~~ I never ~~learned~~ mastered
their smiling ph~~rase~~ for every occasion -
~~t~~hey went their rigid little ways

To meditate in a closet or a trunk
To let l~~ife and~~ unforseen emotion~~s~~
 glance off their glazed complexions

                          To medite in trunk a closet

"Where are the dolls who loved me so . . ."

Where are the dolls who loved me so
when I was young?
Who cared for me with hands of bisque,
poked breadcrumbs in between my lips,

   Where are the early nurses,
Gertrude, Zilpha, and Nokomis?

Through their real eyes   [size]

   blank crotches,
and play wrist-watches,
whose hands moved only when they   wanted—

   Their stoicism I never mastered
their smiling phrase for every occasion—
They went their rigid little ways

To meditate in a closet   or a trunk
To let unforeseen emotions
   glance off their glazed complexions

                            [to meditate in trunks
                                 or closets]

Early 1950s (Vassar 68.2); published in *Edgar Allan Poe & The Juke-Box.*

A Short, Slow Life

I lived in a pocket of Time.
It was close, it was warm.
Along the dark arm of the river
the houses, the lawns, the tiny church,
but little white crosses   in a fluff of
              lost of the willow leaves,   gray
                      and a   gestures
his roots constricted by,   roof,
        Roughly his land worked in,
and tumbled us out.

A Short, Slow Life

We lived in a pocket of Time.
It was close, it was warm.
Along the dark seam of the river
the houses, the barns, the two churches,
hid like white crumbs
in a fluff of gray willows & elms,
till Time made one of his gestures;
his nails scratched the shingled roof.
Roughly his hand reached in,
and tumbled us out.

1950s (Vassar 74.10); published in *Edgar Allan Poe & The Juke-Box*.

SUICIDE OF A (MODERATE) DICTATOR

For Carlos Lacerda

This is a day when truths will out, perhaps;
leak from the dangling telephone ear-phones
sapping the festooned switchboards' strength;
fall from the windows, blow from off the sills,
-the vague, slight unremarkable contents
of emptying ash-trays; rub off on our fingers
like ink from the un-proof-read newspapers,
crocking the way the unfocussed photographs
of crooked faces do that soil our coats,
our tropical-weight coats like slapped-at moths.

Today's a day when those who work
are idling. Those who played must work
and hurry, too, to get it done,
with little dignity or with none.
The newspapers are sold; the kiosk shutters
crash down. But anyway, in the night
the headlines wrote themselves, see, on the streets
and sidewalks everywhere; a sediment's splashed
even to the first floors of apartment houses.

This is a day that's beautiful as well,
and warm and clear. At seven o'clock I saw
the dogs being walked along the famous beach
as usual, in a shiny gray-green dawn,
leaving their paw-prints draining in the wet.
The line of breakers was steady and the pinkish,
~~rainbow in segments~~ (hung) steadily above it.
        segmented rainbow
At eight two ~~little~~ boys were flying kites.

Suicide of a Moderate Dictator

for Carlos Lacerda

This is a day when truths will out, perhaps;—
leak from the dangling telephone ear-phones
sapping the festooned switchboards' strength;
fall from the windows, blow from off the sills,
—the vague, slight unremarkable contents
of emptying ash-trays; rub off on our fingers
like ink from the un-proof-read newspapers,
crocking the way the unfocused photographs
of crooked faces do that soil our coats,
our tropical-weight coats, like slapped-at moths.

Today's a day when those who work
are idling. Those who played must work
and hurry, too, to get it done,
with little dignity or none.
The newspapers are sold; the kiosk shutters
crash down. But anyway, in the night
the headlines wrote themselves, see, on the streets
and sidewalks everywhere; a sediment's splashed
even to the first floors of apartment houses.

This is a day that's beautiful as well,
and warm and clear. At seven o'clock I saw
the dogs being walked along the famous beach
as usual, in a shiny gray-green dawn,
leaving their paw-prints draining in the wet.
The line of breakers was steady and the pinkish,
segmented rainbow steadily hung above it.
At eight two little boys were flying kites.

c. 1954 or after, following the suicide of Getúlio Vargas on August 24, 1954 (Vassar 67.14);
published in *Edgar Allan Poe & The Juke-Box.*

KEATON

I will be good; I will be good.
I have set my small jaw for the ages.
and nothing can distract me from
solivng the appointed emergencies
Even with my small brain
- witness the size of my hat-band the diamter of my hat band
and the depth of the crown of my hat

I will be correct; I know what it is to be a man.
I will be ccorrect or bust.
I will love but not impose my feelings
I will serve and serve
with lute or   I will not say anything.

If the machinery goes, will repair it
If it goes again I will repair it again
My backbone

through these endless etceteras painful

No, it is not the way to be, they say.
Go with the skid, turn always to leeward
and see what happens, I ask you , now

I lost a lovely smile somewhere, ꬰꬰꬰꬰ/ꬰꬰꬰ/
and many colors dropped out
The rigid spine will break, they say -
Bend, bend.

I was made at right angles to the world
and I see it so I can only see it so.
I do not find all this absurdity people talk about
        ; find
Perhaps a paradise   a serious paradise where lovers hold hands
and everything works
    I am not sentimental -

Keaton

I will be good; I will be good.
I have set my small jaw for the ages.
and nothing can distract me from
solving the appointed emergencies
Even with my small brain
—witness the size of my hat-band   the diameter of my hat band
and the depth of the crown of my hat

I will be correct; I know what it is to be a man.
I will be correct or bust.
I will love but not impose my feelings
I will serve and serve
with lute or   I will not say anything.

If the machinery goes, I will repair it
If it goes again I will repair it again
My backbone

through these endless etceteras painful

No, it is not the way to be, they say.
Go with the skid, turn always to leeward
and see what happens, I ask you , now

I lost my lovely smile somewhere,
and many colors dropped out
The rigid spine will break, they say—
Bend, bend.

I was made at right angles to the world
and I see it so   I can only see it so.
I do not find all this absurdity people talk about   [. find]
Perhaps a paradise   a serious paradise where lovers hold hands
and everything works
      I am not sentimental—

n.d. (Vassar 66.11); published in *Edgar Allan Poe & The Juke-Box.*

MIMOSO, NEAR DEATH

?
2'

Mimoso, the donkey
has taken to standing
inside a truck-body,
an old blue truck-body
that's been there for ages,
lying dissolving
in the long grass
on the side of the hill.
All day in the sun
he stands heading up-hill.
In the past week
the grass has turned red,
a fine, quiet fire,
~~the whole hill is red~~
glistening, and silent; ~~/fiery/2/~~
the whole hill is red.

The fires have come down now,
the Captains consumed —

Elijah the Tisbite. —— ?
You are that hairy man
girt with a leather girdle
about your loins

                                   the
(find) The sky-blue chariot
        wheel-less, and (engineless), wafts
        ~~wafts~~

and the tall grass releases
                    seeds

in a whirlwind of grass-seed.

in the (soft
            whirlwind
that blows softly the fiery grasse,
seeding

"thou shalt not come down off
 that bed (that truck bed) on
 the which thou hast gone up
 but) shalt surely die"
But shalt surely go up

the soft whirlwind
waft hoyo upwards
in a cloud of red grass-seeds/

              until
the /fires/ have come down.
the fires have come down now,
the captains are consumed.
~~the fires are come down~~
the fires are come down,
~~the captains~~ consumed.

Mimoso, Mimoso, the fires has come
the red ~~~~ the captains down
                    consumed —

— why are you waiting?
The ~~/fires/ are /come/ down,~~
~~The fires are come down,~~
the captain s consumed.

You are that hairy man
god, — dill your loin
girt with leather girdle

Old sky-blue the chariot
wheel-less (& engineless) —
~~~~ shafted   (wafts)
~~~~ wafts off, the
~~~~

Death of Mimoso

Mimoso the donkey
has taken to standing
inside a truck-body,   [the]
an old blue truck-body
that's been there for ages,
lying dissolving
in the long grass
on the side of the hill.
All day in the sun
he stands, heading up-hill.
In the past week
the grass has turned red,
a fine quiet fire,
glistening, silent;
the whole hill is red.

c. 1959 (Vassar 64.15). An earlier typescript draft was published as "Mimoso, Near Death" in
Edgar Allan Poe & The Juke-Box.

APARTMENT IN LEME

1.

Off to the left, those islands, named and re-named
so many times now everyone's forgotten
their names, are sleeping.

Pale rods of light, the morning's implements,
lie in among them tarnishing already,
just like our knives and forks.

Because we live at your open mouth, oh Sea,
with your cold breath blowing warm, your warm breath cold,
like in the fairy tale.

Not only do you tarnish our knives and forks
- regularly the silver coffee-pot goes into
dark, rainbow-edged eclipse;

the windows blur and mirrors are wet to touch.
Custodia complains, and then you frizz
her straightened, stiffened hair.

Sometimes you embolden, sometimes bore.
You smell of codfish and old rain. Homesick, the salt
weeps in the salt-cellars.

Breathe in. Breathe out. We're so accustomed to
those sounds we only hear them in the night.
Then they come closer

but you keep your distance.

2.

It's growing lighter. On the beach two men
get up from ~~shallow graves of newspaper~~ *shallow* newspaper-lined graves.
A third sleeps on. His coverlet

is corrugated paper, a flattened box.
One running dog, two early bathers, stop
dead in their tracks; detour.

Wisps of fresh green stick to your foamy lips   *foaming*
like those on horses' lips. The sand's bestrewn:
white lilies, broken stalks,

white candles with wet, blackened wicks,
and green glass bottles for white alcohol
meant for the goddess meant to come last night.

(But you've emptied them all.)

Apartment in Leme

1.

Off to the left, those islands, named and re-named
so many times now everyone's forgotten
their names, are sleeping.

Pale rods of light, the morning's implements,
lie in among them tarnishing already,
just like our knives and forks.

Because we live at your open mouth, oh Sea,
with your cold breath blowing warm, your warm breath cold,
like in the fairy tale.

Not only do you tarnish our knives and forks
—regularly the silver coffee-pot goes into
dark, rainbow-edged eclipse;

the windows blur and mirrors are wet to touch.
Custodia complains, and then you frizz
her straightened, stiffened hair.

Sometimes you embolden, sometimes bore.
You smell of codfish and old rain. Homesick, the salt
weeps in the salt-cellars.

Breathe in. Breathe out. We're so accustomed to
those sounds we only hear them in the night.
Then they come closer

but you keep your distance.

2.

It's growing lighter. On the beach two men
get up from shallow, newspaper-lined graves.
A third sleeps on. His coverlet

307

3.

Perhaps she came, at that.   It was so clear!
And you were keeping quiet: ~~Oh,~~ Slightly roughened,
greeny-black, scaly

as one of those corroded old bronze mirrors
in all the world's museums   (How did the ancients
ever see anything in them?),

~~still~~ capable of reflecting the biggest stars.
One cluster, bright, astringent as white currants,
hung from the Magellanic Clouds

above you and the beach and its assorted
lovers and worshippers, almost within their reach
if they had noticed.

The candles flickered. Worshippers, ~~holding hands,~~ dressed in white,
holding hands, singing, walked into you waist-deep.
The ~~And~~ Lovers lay in the sand, embraced.

Far out, the ~~saffron~~ flares of five invisible
fishing boats wobbled and hitched along,
farther ~~away~~ than the stars,

weaker, and older.

4.

But, now the sun. Slowly, ~~as if~~ reluctant~~ly,~~
you let go of it; it as slowly rises,
metallic, two-dimensional.

You sigh, and sigh again. We live at your open mouth,
with your cold breath blowing warm, your warm breath cold
~~as~~ in the fairy tale

-no, ~~is it~~ ~~the~~ legend.

is corrugated paper, a flattened box.
One running dog, two early bathers, stop
dead in their tracks; detour.

Wisps of fresh green stick to your foamy lips   [foaming]
like those on horses' lips. The sand's bestrewn:
white lilies, broken stalks,

white candles with wet, blackened wicks,
and green glass bottles for white alcohol
meant for the goddess meant to come last night.

(But you've emptied them all.)

3.

Perhaps she came, at that. It was so clear!   [—]
And you were keeping quiet: roughened,   [still, rough~~ened~~
greeny-black, scaly   enough,]

as one of those corroded old bronze mirrors
in all the world's museums (How did the ancients
ever see anything in them?),

incapable of reflecting even the biggest stars.
One cluster, bright, astringent as white currants,
hung from the Magellanic Clouds

above you and the beach and its assorted
lovers and worshippers, almost within their reach
if they had noticed.

The candles flickered. Worshippers in white,
holding hands, singing, walked into you waist-deep.
The lovers lay in the sand, embraced.

Far out, saffron flares of five invisible
fishing boats wobbled and hitched along,
farther out than the stars,

weaker and older.

4.

But for now the sun. Slowly, reluctantly,
you let go of it; it as slowly rises,   [you're letting go
metallic, two-dimensional.   of it; it slowly rises:]

You sigh, and sigh again. We live at your open mouth,
with your cold breath blowing warm, your warm breath cold
like in the fairy tale

—no, ~~as in the~~ legend.   [no—the legend.]
                                                         [I mean]

1963 (Vassar 64.19); published in *Edgar Allan Poe & The Juke-Box*.

Dear, my compass
still points north
to wooden houses
and blue eyes,
fairy-tales where
flaxen-headed
younger sons
bring home the goose,
love in hay-lofts,
Protestants, and
heavy drinkers...
Springs are backward,
but crab-apples
ripen to rubies,
cranberries
to drops of blood,
and swans can paddle
icy water,
so hot the blood
in those webbed feet.
— Cold as it is, we'd
go to bed, dear,
early, but never
to keep warm.

"Dear, my compass . . ."

Dear, my compass
still points north
to wooden houses
and blue eyes,
fairy-tales where
flaxen-headed
younger sons
bring home the goose,

love in hay-lofts,
Protestants, and
heavy drinkers . . .
Springs are backward,

but crab-apples
ripen to rubies,
cranberries
to drops of blood,

and swans can paddle
icy water,
so hot the blood
in those webbed feet.
—Cold as it is, we'd
go to bed, dear,
early, but never
to keep warm.

c. 1965 (private collection; photograph courtesy of Carmen Oliveira, with thanks to Barbara Page and Lloyd Schwartz). A second, typed version organizes all the stanzas into quatrains, and was published in *Edgar Allan Poe & The Juke-Box*.

INVENTORY
Bed, birdcage, and a chest of draw drawers,
the biggest shell, the flat and foot-shaped
piece of granite I found myself,
the paddle, and the portable ink-well;

the baby-book, the/coffe spoons the blue enamm the cloisonee
coffe spoons with blue enamel,

                                the living cat
where   - where can I take them next?   wand where
                                do we go next?

Oh let me not have looked
Let it somehow be that I never saw

& the cascade seems hurrying to some
climax, but really never cnages -

Inventory

Bed, birdcage, and a chest of drawers,
the biggest shell, the flat and foot-shaped
piece of granite I found myself,
the paddle, and the portable ink-well;

the baby-book, coffee spoons the blue enamm   the cloisonné
coffee spoons with blue enamel,

                                                              [the living cat
where   —where can I take them next?   and where
                                                          do we go next?]

Oh let me not have looked
Let it somehow be that I never saw

& the cascade seems hurrying to some
climax, but really never changes—

January 1967 (Vassar 66.9); published in *Edgar Allan Poe & The Juke-Box*. In line 11, "changes" is read for "cnages."

A DRUNKARD

When I was three, I watched the Salem fire.
It burned all night (or then I thought it did)
and I stood in my crib & watched it burn.
The sky was bright red; everything was red:
out on the lawn, my mother's white dress looked
rose-red; my white enammelled crib was red.
and my hands holding to its   rods -
the brass knbobs heldspecks of fire
its brass knobs holding specks of fire -

I felt   amazement   not fear
but   amazement   may be
my infancly's main emotion - chief
People were playing hoses on the roofs
 of the summer cottages in Marblehead   on Marblehead neck
the red sky was filled with flying moats,
cinders and coals, and bigger things, scorched black burnt
The water glowed like fire, too, but flat
I watched some boats arriving on our beach
fukk of escaping people (I didn't know that)
One dory, sillhouted black (and later I
thought of this as having looked like
Washington Crossing the Delaware, all black -
in sillhoutte -
I was terribly thirsty but mama didn't hear
me calling her. Ou on the lawn
she and some neighbors were giving coffee
or food or something to the peoplelanding in the boats -
I glimmpsed her once in a while I caught a glimpse of her
and called and called - no one paid any attention -

In the morning acros s the bay brilliant omorning
the fire still went on,but in the sunlight
we saw no more glare, just the clouds of smoke
The beach was strewn with cindess, dark with ash -
strange objects seemed ot have blown across the water
lifted by that terrible heat, through the red sky?
Blackened boards, shiny black like black featehers -
pieces of furniture, parts of boats, and clothes -

I picked up a woman's long black cotton
stocking. Curiosuty. My mother said sharply
Put that down! I remember clearly, clearly -

A Drunkard

When I was three, I watched the Salem fire.
It burned all night (or then I thought it did)
and I stood in my crib & watched it burn.
The sky was bright red; everything was red:
out on the lawn, my mother's white dress looked
rose-red; my white enammelled crib was red.
and my hands   holding to its   rods—
the brass knobs held specks of fire
its brass knobs holding specks of fire—

I felt   amazement   not fear
but   amazement   may be
my infancy's main emotion—chief
People were playing hoses on the roofs
 of the summer cottages in Marblehead   on Marblehead neck
the red sky was filled with flying moats,
cinders and coals, and bigger things, scorched black burnt
The water glowed like fire, too, but flat
I watched some boats arriving on our beach
full of escaping people (I didn't know that)
One dory, silhouetted black (and later I
thought of this as having looked like
Washington Crossing the Delaware, all black—
in silhouette—
I was terribly thirsty but mama didn't hear
me calling her. Out on the lawn
she and some neighbors were giving coffee
or food or something to the people landing in the boats—
I glimpsed her once in a while I caught a glimpse of her
and called and called—no one paid any attention—

In the morning across the bay   brilliant morning
the fire still went on, but in the sunlight
we saw no more glare, just the clouds of smoke
The beach was strewn with cinders, dark with ash—
strange objects seemed to have blown across the water

DRUNKARD - 2.

But since that day, that reprimand
that nigt that day thatreprimand -
I have had a suffered from abnormal thirst -
I swear it's true - and by the age
of twenty or twenty-one I had begun
to drink, & drink - I   can't get enough
and, as you must have noticed,
I'm half-drunk now...

And all I'm telling you may be a lie...

lifted by that terrible heat, through the red sky?
Blackened boards, shiny black like black feathers—
pieces of furniture, parts of boats, and clothes—

I picked up a woman's long black cotton
stocking. Curiosity.   My mother said sharply
Put that down!   I remember clearly, clearly—

But since that day, that reprimand
that night that day that reprimand—
I have had a suffered from abnormal thirst—
I swear it's true—and by the age
of twenty or twenty-one I had begun
to drink, & drink—I   can't get enough
and, as you must have noticed,
I'm half-drunk now . . .

And all I'm telling you may be a lie . . .

c. 1970–1971 (Vassar 64.22); published in *Edgar Allan Poe & The Juke-Box*. Spelling is corrected
and words separated throughout.

THE
Fannie Farmer
COOKBOOK

You won't become a <u>gourmet</u>* cook
By studying on Fannie's book —
Her thoughts on Food & Keeping House
Are scarcely those of Lévi-Strauss.
Nevertheless, you'll find, I rather deem,
The <u>basic elements</u>** are here.
And if a problem should arise:
The Soufflée fall before your eyes,
Or strange things happen to the Rice
— You know I love to give advice.

Elizabeth

* forbidden word
** " " phrase

Christmas, 1971

P.S. Fannie should not be underrated;
She has become sophisticated.
She's picked up many gourmet* tricks
Since the edition of '96.

[Lines written in a copy of Fannie Farmer's *Boston Cooking School Cook Book*, given to Frank Bidart]

You won't become a *gourmet** cook
By studying our Fannie's book—
Her thoughts on Food & Keeping House
Are scarcely those of Levi-Strauss.
Nevertheless, you'll find, Frank dear,
The *basic elements*** are here.
And if a problem should arise:
The Soufflé fall before your eyes,
Or strange things happen to the Rice
—You know I *love* to give advice.

Elizabeth

*forbidden word
** "   " phrase

Christmas, 1971

P.S.   Fannie should not be underrated;
       She has become sophisticated.
       She's picked up many *gourmet** tricks
       Since the edition of '96.

1971 (Houghton bMS Am 2036); published in *Elizabeth Bishop and Her Art* (1983), edited by
Lloyd Schwartz and Sybil P. Estess, and in *The Complete Poems, 1927–1979*. Schwartz asked
Bishop's permission to publish the inscription. She replied, "I suppose it is all right to print
the Fanny Farmer dedication—but perhaps it shd. say, in ( )'s, *A present to Frank Bidart*—or
else a longer title, a la Wordsworth—*'Lines written in a copy of F F's Boston Cooking School Cook
Book, given to Frank Bidart'* . . . ?" (EB to Lloyd Schwartz, dated "August 23rd (I think) 1977,"
Collection of Lloyd Schwartz.)

[Draft 2]

VAGUE POEM/ VAGURE

VAGUE POEM/ VAGUELY LOVE POEM

VAGUE POEM (Vaguely Love Poem)

VAGUE POEM   (Vaguely love poem)

The trip west -
- I think I dreamed that trip.
They talked a lot of "Rose Rocks"
or maybe "Rock Roses"
- I'm not sure now, but someone tried to get me some.
(And two or three students had.)

She said she had some at her house.
They were at the door, she said.   They were by the back door, she said.
- A ramshackle house.
An Army house ? - No, a Navy house; Yes,
for inland   that far inland.
But there was nothing but dirt -   There was nothing by the back door but dirt
or that same monochrome, (dry) sepia straw, I'd seen everywhere.
Oh she said the dog has carried them off.
(A big black dog, female, was running around us.)
                    dancing

Later, as we drank tea from mugs, she found one,
"a sort of one". "This one is just beginning. See -
you can see here, it's beginning to look like a rose.
It's - well, a crystal, crystals form-
I don't know any geology myself..."
(And Neither did I.)
Faintly, I could make out - perhaps - in the dull,
rose-red lump of soil (apparently)?
a rose-like shape; faint glitters... Yes, perhaps
there was a magic crystal at work inside.
            secret, powerful

I almost saw it: turning into a rose
without any of the intervening
roots, stem, buds, and so on; just
earth to rose and back again.

(Crystalography and its laws: totally
until I found something I wanted to study once until I learned   I once wanted to study,
that it would involve a lot of arithmetic, mathematics, (that is,.)

Just now, when I saw you naked again,
I thought the same words: rose-rock; rock-rose...
Rose, trying, working, to show itself,
(unimaginable connections, unseen, shining edges,
forming, folding over,]
Rose-rock, unformed, flesh beginning, crystal by crystal,
is clear pink breasts and darker, crystalline nipples,
rose-rock, rose-quartz, roses, roses, roses,
exacting roses from the body,
and the even darker, accurate, rose of sex -

Vague Poem (*Vaguely love poem*)

The trip west—
—I think I *dreamed* that trip.
They talked a lot of "Rose Rocks"
or maybe "Rock Roses"
—I'm not sure now, but someone tried to get me some.
(And two or three students had.)

She said she had some at her house.
They were by the back door, she said.
—A ramshackle house.
An Army house ?—No, "a *Navy* house." Yes,
                                    that far inland.
There was nothing by the back door but dirt
or that same dry monochrome, sepia straw I'd seen everywhere.
Oh she said the dog has carried them off.
(A big black dog, female, was dancing around us.)

Later, as we drank tea from mugs, she found one,
"a sort of one". "This one is just beginning. See—
you can see here, it's beginning to look like a rose.
It's—well, a crystal, crystals form–
I don't know any geology myself . . ."
(Neither did I.)
Faintly, I could make out—perhaps—in the dull,
rose-red lump of, apparently, soil,
a rose-like shape; faint glitters . . .   Yes, perhaps
there was a secret, powerful crystal at work inside.

I *almost* saw it: turning into a rose
without any of the intervening
roots, stem, buds, and so on; just
earth to rose and back again.
Crystalography and its laws:
something I   I once wanted badly to study,
until I learned that it would involve a lot of arithmetic, that is,
        mathematics.

Just now, when I saw you naked again,
I thought the same words: rose-rock; rock-rose . . .
Rose, trying, working to show itself,
forming, folding over,
unimaginable connections, unseen, shining edges.
Rose-rock, unformed, flesh beginning, crystal by crystal,
clear pink breasts and darker, crystalline nipples,
rose-rock, rose-quartz, roses, roses, roses,
exacting roses from the body,
and the even darker, accurate, rose of sex—

c. 1973? (Vassar, 67.23); published in *Edgar Allan Poe & The Juke-Box.*

Breakfast Song

My love, my saving grace,
your eyes are awfully blue.
I kiss your funny face,
your coffee-flavoured mouth.
Last night I slept with you.
Today I love you so
how can I bear to go
(as soon I must, I know)
to bed with ugly death
in that cold, filthy place,
to sleep there without you,
without the ~~close, sweet breath~~   ~~steady breath~~   *easy?*
and nightlong, limblong warmth   *peaceful breath?*
I've grown ~~accustomed~~ (to?
— Nobody ~~wants to die~~;
tell me it is a lie!
But no, I know it's true.
It's just the common case;
there's nothing one can do.
My love, my saving grace,
your eyes are ~~early~~ blue awfully
+ instant ~~and~~ ~~truly~~ blue   *awfully?*
(early)

Breakfast Song

My love, my saving grace,
your eyes are awfully blue.
I kiss your funny face,
your coffee-flavored mouth.
Last night I slept with you.
Today I love you so
how can I bear to go
(as soon I must, I know)
to bed with ugly death
in that cold, filthy place,
to sleep there without you,
without the easy breath
and nightlong, limblong warmth
I've grown accustomed to?
—Nobody wants to die;
tell me it is a lie!
But no, I know it's true.
It's just the common case;
there's nothing one can do.
My love, my saving grace,
your eyes are awfully blue
early & instant blue

c. 1973–1974. Collection of Lloyd Schwartz; published in *Edgar Allan Poe & The Juke-Box*. The manuscript is in Lloyd Schwartz's hand, copied from Bishop's notebook on or around January 3, 1974. The notebook does not survive, but a surviving typescript draft of a poem entitled "Simple-Minded Morning Song," consisting of two lines—"My love, my saving grace, / your eyes are very blue."—is in Bishop's papers (Vassar 64.24).

FOR A GRANDFATHER

How far north are you by now?
—(But I'm almost close enough to see you.):
Under the North Star,
   stocky, broadbacked & determined,
   trudging on splaying snowshoes
   over the snow's hard, brilliant, curdled crust...
Aurora Borealis burns in silence.
Streamers of red, of purple,
   make flecks of color on your bald head.
Where is your sealskin cap with ear-lugs?
That old fur coat with the black frogs?
You'll catch your death again.

If I should overtake you, kiss your cheek,
~~and kiss your cheek,~~
   its silver stubble would feel like hoar-frost
   and your old-fashioned, walrus moustaches
   be hung with icicles.

Creak, creak... frozen thongs and creaking snow.
(I think these drifts are endless; as far as the Pole
   they hold no shadows but their own, and ours.
~~Please, Grandpa,~~ stop! I haven't been this cold in years.
Grandfather, please!

[Draft 4]

For Grandfather

How far north are you by now?
—But I'm almost close enough to see you:
under the North Star,
stocky, broadbacked & determined,
trudging on splaying snowshoes
over the snow's hard, brilliant, curdled crust . . .
Aurora Borealis burns in silence.
Streamers of red, of purple,
fleck with color your bald head.
Where is your sealskin cap with ear-lugs?
That old fur coat with the black frogs?
You'll catch your death again.

If I should overtake you, kiss your cheek,
its silver stubble would feel like hoar-frost
and your old-fashioned, walrus moustaches
be hung with icicles.

Creak, creak . . . frozen thongs and creaking snow.
These drifts are endless, I think; as far as the Pole
they hold no shadows but their own, and ours.
Grandfather, please stop! I haven't been this cold in years.

Mid-1970s? (Vassar 65.19); published in *Edgar Allan Poe & The Juke-Box.*

SALEM WILLOWS

Oh, Salem Willows,
where I rode a golden lion
around and around and around,
king of the carrousel
and the other golden creatures,
around and around and around,
sumptuosly, slowly,
to the ~~loud, dogmatic~~ music
of the gold calliope.

Round went the golden camel
and the high gold elephant
with his small red velvet rug,
around and around and around;
the staid, two-seated chariot,
gold horses and gold tigers,
~~but~~ I preferred the lion.
~~and~~ mounted him astride.

~~There was a flimsy rein.~~
His gold mane was abundant.
His mouth was open; ~~his~~ tongue
enameled red; his eyes
brown glass with golden sparkles.
~~He'd lifted his~~ right forepaw
but the others wouldn't budge.

~~At~~ the center, ~~statues stood~~
~~around the calliope:~~
front halves of plaster people.
From time to time, to the music,
they'd raise a flute, but never
quite to their lips; they'd almost
beat their drums; they'd not quite
pluck their upheld lyres.
It was as if that music,
~~mechanical,~~
discouraged them from trying.

Around and around and round.
~~Had we all been~~ touched by Midas?
Were we a ring of Saturn,
adizzy,   nimbus?
Or were we one of the crowns
the saints "cast down" (but why?)
"upon the glassy sea"?
The carrousel slowed down.
Really, beyond the willows,
glittered a glassy sea
and Aunt Maud sat and knitted
and knitted, waiting for me.

Salem Willows

Oh, Salem Willows,
where I rode a golden lion
around and around and around,
king of the carrousel
and the other golden creatures,
around and around and around,
sumptuously, slowly,
to the coarse, mechanical music
of the gold calliope!

Round went the golden camel
and the high gold elephant
with his small red velvet rug,
around and around and around;
the staid, two-seated chariot,
gold horses and gold tigers,
I preferred the lion.   [but above all others and]
I mounted him astride.

His gold mane was abundant   [wooden mane was golden]
His mouth was open; his tongue
enameled red; his eyes
brown glass with golden sparkles.
His right forepaw was lifted
but the others wouldn't budge.

                                                                            [<?]
At the center,   [There were figures
front halves, plaster people.   at the center—]

From time to time, to the music,
they'd raise a flute, but never
quite to their lips; they'd almost
beat their drums; they'd not quite
pluck their upheld lyres.
It was as if that music,

331

                    mechanical, loud,   [(stern &)]
discouraged them from trying.   [coarse, mechanical,
                                                                    loud—]
Around and around and around.   [mechanical, loud—]
Were we all touched by Midas?
Were we a ring of Saturn,
a dizzy,   nimbus?   [turning?]
Or were we one of the crowns
the saints "cast down" (but why?)
"upon the glassy sea"?
The carrousel slowed down.
Really, beyond the willows,
glittered a glassy sea
and Aunt Maud sat and knitted
and knitted, waiting for me.

1970s (Vassar 67.7); published in *Edgar Allan Poe & The Juke-Box*.

FLORIDA REVISITED

At first I took it for a bird
lying ~~dead~~ at the water's edge,
wreathed in a little tan-colored foam
by the ~~low receding wave~~ tide
- a dead black bird. No. The breast of one?
No. Then it must be a single wing,
coal-black, ~~glistening~~ blue-and-black
like coal, with each wet feather ~~quite~~ distinct:
scapulars, secondaries and primaries,
soaked and separate, catching light.

I picked it up. It wasn't a bird.
A bird, or its heart, or a wing, ~~much~~
would have been light; ~~but~~ this was lighter.
(~~that~~ sensation-like stepping down
when there is no step.)
It was only a fragment of charred wood,
feather-light, feather-marked , _almost dry,_
- not a bird at all.

The sun, in "winter quarters"
was dropping into the Gulf

And, Incredibly,
a man ~~sitting~~ on the beach,
~~was~~ making a movie of it.
The sun seemed to be setting to oblige him.
His camera ~~gave a~~ tiny click-click-click
-~~click~~. The ~~sun went a little lower.~~ sun~~set~~   _&a perfect — th sun_
Did he think it was the last one in the world?

~~Did he still to what to record it~~
~~a the last one in the world?~~

elaborating

improving

highly —

Was it the last one in the world
that he thought he had to record it ?

Florida Revisited

At first I took it for a bird
lying at the water's edge,
wreathed in a little tan-colored foam
by the tide   [tide]   [ebbing
—a dead black bird. No. The breast of one?   tide—]
No. Then it must be a single wing,
coal-black, glistening blue-and-black
like coal, with each wet feather distinct:
scapulars, secondaries and primaries,
soaked and separate, catching light.

I picked it up. It wasn't a bird.
A bird or its heart or a wing
would have been light; this was much lighter.
(That sensation—like stepping down
when there is no step.)
It was only a fragment of charred wood,
feather-light, feather-marked, almost dry,
—not a bird at all.

The sun, in "winter quarters"
was dropping into the Gulf

And, Incredibly,
a man was on the beach
making a *movie* of it.
The sun seemed to be setting to oblige him.
His camera gave out tiny *click-click-click
-click*s. The ~~sun went a little lower.~~ sun~~set~~   [In a perfect—the sun]
Did he think it was the last one in the world?

335

[elaborating]
[improving]
　　[display—]

[Was it the last one in the world
that he thought he had to record it?]

c. 1976 (Vassar 64.24); an earlier draft was published in *Edgar Allan Poe & The Juke-Box.*

APPENDIX II: Contents of Elizabeth Bishop's Books of Poetry on First Publication, 1946–1977

The most dramatic changes between editions are to the order of poems and the omission of some content. Bishop revised individual poems minimally between books, rewording or reshaping in a few instances half a line or three. In addition, she added dedications, corrected misprints, and changed punctuation—periods, commas, and dashes, and, most frequently, hyphens (omitted or added). All the variants between editions are noted in Candace W. MacMahon's *Elizabeth Bishop: A Bibliography, 1927–1979* (Charlottesville: Bibliographical Society of University of Virginia, University of Virginia Press, 1980). This edition follows *The Complete Poems* (1969) and *Geography III* (1976); the notes list only instances in which the texts differ in wording from the first book publications or where a revision published in *The Complete Poems, 1927–1979* (1983) has been adopted.

NORTH & SOUTH (HOUGHTON MIFFLIN, 1946)

The Map; The Imaginary Iceberg; Casabianca; The Colder the Air; Wading at Wellfleet; Chemin de Fer; The Gentleman of Shalott; Large Bad Picture; From the Country to the City; The Man-Moth; Love Lies Sleeping; A Miracle for Breakfast;[1] The Weed; The Unbeliever, The Monument, Paris, 7 A.M., Quai D'Orleans," Sleeping on the Ceiling; Sleeping Standing Up; Cirque D'Hiver; Florida; Jerónimo's House; Roosters; Seascape; Little Exercise;[3] The Fish; Late Air; Cootchie; Songs for a Colored Singer;[4] Anaphora[5]

POEMS: NORTH & SOUTH—A COLD SPRING
(HOUGHTON MIFFLIN, 1955)

NORTH & SOUTH

The Map; The Imaginary Iceberg; Casabianca; The Colder the Air; Wading at Wellfleet; Chemin de Fer; The Gentleman of Shalott; Large Bad Picture; From the Country to the City; The Man-Moth; Love Lies Sleeping; A Miracle for Breakfast; The Weed; The Unbeliever; The Monument; Paris, 7 A.M.; Quai D'Orleans; Sleeping on the Ceiling; Sleeping Standing Up; Cirque D'Hiver; Florida; Jerónimo's House; Roosters; Seascape; Little Exercise; The Fish; Late Air; Cootchie; Songs for a Colored Singer; Anaphora

A COLD SPRING

A Cold Spring; Over 2,000 Illustrations and a Complete Concordance; The Bight; A Summer's Dream; Cape Breton; At the Fishhouses;[6] View of The Capitol from The Library of Congress; Insomnia; The Prodigal; Faustina, or Rock Roses; Varick Street; Four Poems; Argument; Letter to N.Y.; The Mountain;[7] Invitation to Miss Marianne Moore; Arrival at Santos;[8] The Shampoo

POEMS (CHATTO & WINDUS, 1956)

The Map; The Colder the Air; The Imaginary Iceberg; Wading at Wellfleet; The Man-Moth; Large Bad Picture; The Unbeliever; The Weed; Cirque D'Hiver; Sleeping Standing Up; Roosters; The Fish; Little Exercise; Letter to N.Y.; A Cold Spring; At the Fishhouses; The Bight; Faustina, or Rock Roses; The Prodigal; Invitation to Miss Marianne Moore

QUESTIONS OF TRAVEL (FARRAR, STRAUS AND GIROUX, 1965)

I. BRAZIL

Arrival at Santos; Brazil, January 1, 1502; Questions of Travel; Squatter's Children; Manuelzinho; Electrical Storm; Song for the Rainy Season;[9] The Armadillo; The River-man; Twelfth Morning; or What You Will; The Burglar of Babylon[10]

II. ELSEWHERE

In the Village (a story);[11] Manners; Sestina; First Death in Nova Scotia; Filling Station; Sunday, 4 A.M.; Sandpiper;[12] From Trollope's Journal; Visits to St. Elizabeths[13]

SELECTED POEMS (CHATTO & WINDUS, 1967)[14]

From NORTH & SOUTH

The Map; The Imaginary Iceberg; The Colder the Air; From the Country to the City; The Man-Moth; A Miracle for Breakfast; Large Bad Picture; The Monument; Cirque D'Hiver; Florida; Jerónimo's House; The Fish; Cootchie; Songs for a Colored Singer; Roosters

From A COLD SPRING

Over 2,000 Illustrations and a Complete Concordance; The Bight; Faustina, or Rock Roses; A Summer's Dream; Cape Breton; At the Fishhouses; The Prodigal; Varick Street; Two Poems;[15] Invitation to Miss Marianne Moore; The Shampoo

From QUESTIONS OF TRAVEL

I. Brazil

Arrival at Santos; Brazil, January 1, 1502; Questions of Travel; Squatter's Children; Manuelzinho; Electrical Storm; Song for the Rainy Season; The Armadillo; The River-man; Twelfth Morning; or What You Will; The Burglar of Babylon

II. Elsewhere

Manners; Sestina; First Death in Nova Scotia; Filling Station; Sandpiper; From Trollope's Journal; Visits to St. Elizabeths[16]

THE BALLAD OF THE BURGLAR OF BABYLON
(FARRAR, STRAUS AND GIROUX, 1968)[17]

Introduction; The Ballad of the Burglar of Babylon

THE COMPLETE POEMS (FARRAR, STRAUS AND GIROUX, 1969; CHATTO & WINDUS, 1970)

NORTH & SOUTH

The Map; The Imaginary Iceberg; Casabianca; The Colder the Air; Wading at Wellfleet; Chemin de Fer; The Gentleman of Shalott; Large Bad Picture; From the Country to the City; The Man-Moth; Love Lies Sleeping; A Miracle for Breakfast; The Weed; The Unbeliever; The Monument, Paris, 7 A.M.; Quai D'Orleans; Sleeping on the Ceiling; Sleeping Standing Up; Cirque D'Hiver; Florida; Jerónimo's House; Roosters; Seascape; Little Exercise; The Fish; Late Air; Cootchie; Songs for a Colored Singer; Anaphora

A COLD SPRING

A Cold Spring; Over 2,000 Illustrations and a Complete Concordance; The Bight; A Summer's Dream; At the Fishhouses; Cape Breton; View of The Capitol from The Library of Congress; Insomnia; The Prodigal; Faustina, or Rock Roses; Varick Street; Four Poems; Letter to N.Y.; Argument; Invitation to Miss Marianne Moore; The Shampoo

QUESTIONS OF TRAVEL

I. Brazil

Arrival at Santos; Brazil, January 1, 1502; Questions of Travel; Squatter's Children; Manuelzinho; Electrical Storm; Song for the Rainy Season; The Armadillo; The Riverman; Twelfth Morning; or What You Will; The Burglar of Babylon

II. Elsewhere

Manners; Sestina; First Death in Nova Scotia; Filling Station; Sunday, 4 A.M.; Sandpiper; From Trollope's Journal

III. Translations from the Portuguese

Carlos Drummond de Andrade: Seven-Sided Poem; Don't Kill Yourself; Travelling in the Family; The Table;[18] João Cabral de Melo Neto: From The Death and Life of a Severino

New and Uncollected Work

Rainy Season; Sub-Tropics; The Hanging of the Mouse; Some Dreams They Forgot; Song; House Guest; Trouvée; Going to the Bakery;[19] Under the Window: Ouro Prêto

GEOGRAPHY III (FARRAR, STRAUS AND GIROUX, 1976; CHATTO & WINDUS, 1977)

In the Waiting Room; Crusoe in England;[20] Night City; The Moose; 12 O'Clock News; Poem; One Art; The End of March; Objects & Apparitions; Five Flights Up

NOTES

1. In line 32, "made for me a miracle" became "made for me by a miracle" in *Poems: North & South—A Cold Spring* (1955).
2. A dedication to Margaret Miller was added in *The Complete Poems*.
3. A dedication to Thomas Edwards Manning was added in *The Complete Poems*.
4. Lines 15–17 of section I
   > *and find it very hard*
   > *that all we got for all his dollars and cents*
   > *'s a pile of bottles by the fence*

   were rewritten to read:
   > *and find it very hard.*
   > *What have we got for all his dollars and cents?*
   > *—A pile of bottles by the fence.*

   in *The Complete Poems*. In section II, line 5
   > *'cause this occasion's all his fault.*

   was rewritten to read
   > *this occasion's all his fault.*
5. A dedication in memory of Marjorie Carr Stevens was added in *The Complete Poems*.
6. A comma was added to the end of line 4 in *The Complete Poems, 1927–1979* (a change not followed in this edition).
7. Omitted from the paperback edition (1965) and from *The Complete Poems*.
8. In the *Questions of Travel* (1965) version, a misprint of "self-pitying, mountains" in line 3 was corrected to read "self-pitying mountains." Line 5,
   > *with a little church on top of one. And some warehouses*

   became
   > *with a little church on top of one. And warehouses*

   Line 26,
   > *a retired police lieutenant, and six feet tall,*

   became
   > *a retired police lieutenant, six feet tall,*

   Line 31,
   > *and leave us our Scotch and cigarettes.*

   became
   > *and leave us our bourbon and cigarettes.*

   Also, the subscript "January 1952" was added. In her instructions to the publisher of *Complete Poems*, Bishop wrote, "'Arrival at Santos' should, of course, be used only once. . . . I would like to have it appear in the *Questions of Travel* section, in the version it appears in in *Questions of Travel*" (EB to Michael di Capua and Cynthia Muser, September 21, 1968, copies at Vassar and The New York Public Library).
9. A subscript "Síto da Alcobaçinha, Fazenda Samambaia, Petrópolis" was added in *The Complete Poems, 1927–1979*.
10. In line 112, the misprint of "out at the sea" was corrected to read "out at sea," and an extra gap between stanzas 43 and 44 (setting off the final four stanzas) was closed in *The Complete Poems*. An extra gap between stanzas 45 and 46 (setting off the final two stanzas, which was Bishop's wish) was added in *The Complete Poems, 1927–1979*.
11. Omitted from *The Complete Poems* but proposed for inclusion in an edition of her prose that Bishop contemplated entitling *In the Village & Other Stories* or *In the Village: Stories and Essays*.

12. Line 13:
    > The world is a mist. The world is uniquely

    was rewritten to read

    > The world is a mist. And then the world is

    in *The Complete Poems*.
13. A subscript "November, 1951" was omitted in *The Complete Poems*.
14. The selection was made by Elizabeth Bishop. In a letter published in *The Times Literary Supplement*, Bishop responded to complaints that Chatto & Windus had omitted "In the Village" from her *Selected Poems*: "It is true that the publishers did not choose to include a story that appeared in my last volume of poems published in the United States. However, I was entirely responsible for the selection of poems. It is possible I was over-fussy" (Elizabeth Bishop to the Editor, *TLS*, February 15, 1968, p. 157).
15. "Rain Towards Morning" and "While Someone Telephones."
16. A subscript dated "November, 1951" is omitted in *The Complete Poems*.
17. With woodcuts by Ann Grifalconi.
18. In line 236, "What nothing" was revised to read "But no!" (to better reflect the Portuguese "Qual nada") in *The Complete Poems, 1927–1979*. Bishop wrote this change in the margin of Eamon Grennan's copy of *The Complete Poems* (1969, sixth printing 1978), and initialed the change.
19. A revision of "Oh, poor habit!" to "Oh, mean habit!" in the penultimate line was included in *The Complete Poems, 1927–1979*.
20. In line 24, "over-lapping" became "overlapping" in *The Complete Poems, 1927–1979* (the second change not followed in the present edition). In Bishop's own copy of *Geography III*, she canceled "the" in line 173 ("the shrivelled shoes") and wrote "those?" in the margin, but the change was not adopted in *The Complete Poems, 1927–1979*.

Index of Titles and First Lines

Page numbers in *italics* refer to illustrations.